That's My Story Too

Lessons and Activities for
52 Counselor-Recommended Children's Books

Written by:
Kate Brambrut, MA, NCC &
Amy Sauder Lehman, MA, LPC

youth light inc.

© 2010 by YouthLight, Inc.
Chapin, SC 29036

Design and Layout by
Amy Rule

Project Editing by
Susan Bowman

ISBN: 9781598500820

Library of
Congress Number
2010920668

10 9 8 7 6 5 4 3 2 1
Printed in the
United States

Acknowledgments

Writing this book has been an enjoyable yet enormous undertaking. It would not have been possible without the ongoing support of my friends and family. I would especially like to thank the following people:

- My amazing husband, Marc, who has been my biggest supporter since the conception of the book. He has been my cheerleader, my editor, my sounding board and the giver of many an encouraging hug along the way.
- My parents, Robert and Gail Joiner. Not only did they instill a love for words in me at an early age, but they have always supported my goals and dreams, no matter how big or small.
- My friend and co-writer Amy, who shares my passion for counseling children and for children's books. I think we make a great team!
- The many incredible school counselors and teachers I have worked with and met along the way. I have worked side-by-side with some and have merely met others in passing, but all have inspired me in some way and have shared many great ideas and resources. Thanks especially to Fairfax County Public Schools in Virginia – I am so fortunate to have started my counseling career in such a wonderful school system.
- Judy Thompson – for teaching me that you can get through any challenge in life with the right attitude. Your passion for life, your unwavering support, and your eternal optimism is a constant source of inspiration.

- Kate Brambrut, MA, NCC

I would like to thank the following people for all of their love and support:

- My parents, Clair and Doris Sauder. Thank you, thank you, thank you for instilling the love of reading in me at such an early age and for being 110% supportive of me along the way.
- My husband, Ted. I could not ask for a better confidant and editor-in-chief.
- My co-author, Kate. I am so glad our paths crossed in grad school. It has been such a blessing to share my professional and personal life with you.
- My principal, Mary Shannon, for your unwavering encouragement and support, not only with this book, but also in my overall professional growth as a counselor.
- My LPC supervisor, Elaine Rhymers. Your encouragement, advice and sense of humor kept me inspired during the long road toward my LPC.
- My friends and family, for being the best cheerleaders a girl could ask for!

- Amy E. Sauder Lehman, MA, LPC

Dedications

I would like to dedicate this book to my son Ben, whose early passion for books and words has turned him into quite a talker! He is the kindest and happiest child any mom could ask for and there are no words for how he has changed my life. I am truly blessed. His infectious laughter, enormous smiles and warm hugs got me through many days when I didn't think I could come up with one more idea or write one more word.   *– Kate*

I would like to dedicate this book to the many educators who have deeply enriched my life, both personally and professionally. Your "lessons" have made me a better teacher, counselor, wife, mother and friend. I am grateful. A special dedication goes to my teacher, Ms. Frey, who helped me publish my first "book" back in the fifth grade – you made quite an impression on a young girl.   *– Amy*

Table of Contents

Table of Contents

Table of Contents

Introduction

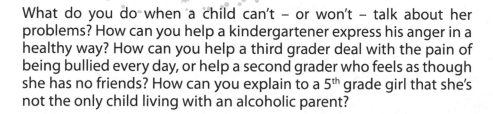

What do you do when a child can't – or won't – talk about her problems? How can you help a kindergartener express his anger in a healthy way? How can you help a third grader deal with the pain of being bullied every day, or help a second grader who feels as though she has no friends? How can you explain to a 5th grade girl that she's not the only child living with an alcoholic parent?

Anyone who interacts with children knows the power of a good book. Books have the unique ability to provoke imagination, stimulate problem solving, create safe havens and promote meaningful conversation. Books can not only transport children to another world, but can also give them the courage, support and encouragement they need to feel safe and secure in the world they're in. Using books as a medium to help children who are experiencing difficulties is what Bibliotherapy is all about. It's about the spark in a child's eye, the "aha" moment when you can see that a child has truly identified with the book character or situation, and has realized he's not alone in his problem.

This book is intended to serve as a resource for anyone who works with children, including the heartbroken parent whose child complains of being bullied at school, the busy school counselor that needs to address anger management in a small group, and the teacher that sees a trend of dishonesty in her classroom.

We have organized the book according to topic. The chapters are broken down by topic area, and within each topic area (grief, bullying, friendship, etc.) are 4 books centered on the particular topic. Accompanying each book, you will find detailed lesson plans, objectives, discussion questions and extension activities. For each book included, we have indicated what age and grade level the book would be most appropriate for, and we have also indicated whether the book is best used one-on-one, in small groups or in classroom guidance. We know that time is a scarce commodity these days, so we have tried our best to make the book as user-friendly and efficient as possible.

When we first came up with the idea for this book, we intended it to be a resource for school counselors – however, as we started discussing the details and layout of the book, we realized the books we were including, along with our discussion questions and extension activities, could just as easily be used between teacher and student, and parent and child. Whoever you are, and whatever your role with children, we hope this book will serve as a helpful resource for years to come.

Ten Steps for Implementing Bibliotherapy

A. Develop a trusting rapport with the child.

B. Consult with school colleagues for additional support

C. Gain support from the child's parents/guardians

D. Identify the child's problem

E. List goals and extension activities for the book

F. Locate the appropriate book

G. Find a creative way to introduce the book to the child

H. Read the book.

I. Complete post-reading activities

J. Assess the impact of the book on the student.

(Prater, 2006)

The History and Advantages of Bibliotherapy

The therapeutic impact of literature is as old as words themselves, but the term bibliotherapy is credited to Samuel Crothers, who first used the word in an article in Atlantic Monthly in 1916. The term described a technique of prescribing books to patients who needed help understanding their problems. The practice of bibliotherapy was initially limited to hospitals, where it was used in addition to the library services provided to World War I veterans. By 1940, bibliotherapy had spread to a variety of settings, and in 1946 it was used for the first time with children [(Agnes, 1946, pp. 8-16). Agnes, S. M. "Bibliotherapy for Socially Maladjusted Children," Catholic Educational Review, 44, 1946, pp. 8-16].

Dale Elizabeth Pehrsson, a professor at the University of Nevada Las Vegas, elaborated more recently, defining "Developmental Bibliotherapy" as the use of bibliotherapy in the educational (i.e. classroom) setting, and using the term "Clinical Bibliotherapy" to refer to bibliotherapy that meets specific counseling goals (2007).

Whether in the classroom or in the counselor's office, books are proven to open the doors of communication between counselors and students, teachers and students, and parents and children alike. They give words to feelings that cannot be expressed, and they allow children an opportunity to see how other people cope with problems the children themselves are having. Anita Iaquinta, Ed.D, an Assistant Professor in the School of Education and Social Sciences at Robert Morris University, recently proved in her research that Bibliotherapy has a positive effect on children's self-esteem, reading readiness and academic achievement (2006).

Bibliotherapy is so effective because children can relate to characters in literature, whose experiences validate the problems and situations children are facing, when they might not ordinarily be able to talk about their problems. Since reading books and listening to stories is something children are very accustomed to, books provide a great comfort zone for delving into topics that can often be very difficult for children to talk about. The process of sorting through all the various emotions that come with a parents' divorce might be overwhelming for a child, yet if the topic of divorce is addressed through a story – with a character the child can identify with – this often gives children courage and strength to tell their own story. As Mary Taylor Rycik explains in her article *9/11 to the Iraq War: Using Books to Help Children Understand Troubled Times*, bibliotherapy is very effective with children who are coping with grief or loss. Books reassure them that some sort of normalcy and routine will be established again (2006).

As children learn they're not alone in experiencing their specific problem, they often learn clever and creative ways to deal with their problem. We have lost count of the number of times we've been reading a story to a child, or to a group of children, and have heard them say, "he's just like me," or "that's exactly what happened to me," or "I felt the same way when that happened." Dr. Iaquinta's research demonstrates that bibliotherapy provides children the opportunity to learn from the main character's problem and then apply the same problem-solving strategies to their own situation. Children also learn that there are several solutions to any given problem, and this often gives them the hope and confidence they need to tackle their problem head on (2006).

Dale Elizabeth Pehrsson warns that students who are intimidated by an academic setting may be "scared" of books. Counselors and teachers will need to communicate the differences between bibliotherapy and class work, being careful to assure students that nothing will be graded, and that there are no right or wrong answers. If the student is a "fearful reader," the counselor should read the book aloud instead of partner reading (2007).

While teachers or counselors may be tempted to exclude all but the most literate or verbal students from bibliotherapy techniques, Mary Ann Prater advises in her book, *Using Children's Books as Bibliotherapy for At-Risk Students: A Guide for Teachers*, that bibliotherapy allows otherwise-underachieving students the opportunity to see books in a new light (2006). Bibliotherapy also works well for children of all ages. Perhsson writes that it is well-suited for pre-adolescents or tweens because they typically aren't developmentally ready for traditional talk therapy, yet they feel too old for play therapy (2007).

How to Implement Bibliotherapy

Implementing bibliotherapy doesn't require a special license or training. It can be as brief or as involved as you choose to make it. You can tailor it to fit a 45-minute classroom guidance session, a 30-minute small group session, or an individual discussion between parent and child. Bibliotherapy is free if you use the public library or your school library. Bibliotherapy can also be easily integrated into language arts class. This is a crucial selling point for teachers, who are always searching for ways to build language skills with their students. All you need is the ability to help children make connections between themselves and the characters in the books. After all, that's the whole point of bibliotherapy!

To facilitate the connections between students and characters, Dr. Iaquinta suggests that teachers, counselors or parents ask themselves the following series of questions before choosing a book for bibliotherapy work:

- Is the story easy to understand and believable?

- Does the book match the student's developmental level?

  - Be sure to allow enough time for children to process the discussion questions – again, know your group. If you're using a book for classroom guidance in second grade, for example, you will likely need a lot more time to process the discussion questions than you would if you're using the same book in a small group of four.

- Does the story address the needs of the student?

  - We can't stress enough the importance of "pre-reading" books with your specific audience in mind. Consider your audience carefully - if the book character's grandmother dies, look at the students in the class to identify students that may have had similar experiences, and consider whether your story might be more appropriate to share in an individual or small group setting. If you are a school counselor and the book deals with a controversial topic, it's also important to know your district's policy on discussing these topics in class.

- Does the story use culturally-sensitive language and avoid gender bias?

  - Consider the ethnicity and socioeconomic level of the book characters - can your audience identify with them? There's nothing worse than thinking you've found the perfect book to use with a child, or group of children, only to have the book "fall flat" with children because they can't relate to the characters.

  - If you are working with a child whose first language is not English, consider using books on tape in the student's native language – this is a great way to ensure that you connect with all students. (Sullivan and Strang 2002).

- At the end of the book, do the characters utilize positive coping mechanisms and come to an agreeable resolution?

- When appropriate, invite parental involvement by sending home copies of the reading so parents can engage their child in conversation (Sullivan and Strang, 2002).

Books on a Budget

Considering the fact that new children's books are published every day, and that the average cost of a children's book is around $10 dollars, it's often not feasible to buy all the books you want or need to work with children. Although we have bought quite a few of the books we're recommending, we have bought very few of them brand new, and we have checked out many from our school library or public library. Here are some other budget friendly sources for books:

- **Get to know your libraries!** This is our favorite place for books. Not only are books free, but libraries have a wide selection, and you can get books quickly. We can't count the number of times we've stopped by our public libraries to check out a book the night before we needed to use it – or the number of times we've checked out a book from the school library just before we needed it for a lesson. Most school librarians also have a "new book" budget to pull from each year, and they are happy to order books that you suggest.

- **Major bookstores offering teacher discounts.** Most national chain bookstores offer an educator discount ranging from 10%-15% - and these bookstores often raise the educator discount to 20% two weeks each year – typically once in the fall and once in the spring.

- **Discount stores.** Stores like *TJ Maxx®*, *Ross® Stores*, and *Marshall's®* are excellent sources for brand new books – especially picture books to use with younger students.

- **Goodwill or Salvation Army**. Books are always a bargain here, and you have the added benefit of knowing your money is going to a good cause!

- **Yard sales.** These are excellent sources for tried and true children's books.

- **Book swaps with other counselors in your area.** Or if you are lucky enough to have a counselor in your area who is retiring, he or she can be a great source for books!

- **Counseling books that come in a series or set.** Typically, books that are purchased as a set will all be based on the same general topic, while those that are purchased as a series will include a variety of different topics. Some popular set books are:

    - *Good Citizenship Counts*, (K-4) – includes 10 individual books that address developing good character and good citizenship

    - *A Rainbow of Hope*, (K-5) – includes 10 individual "storybooklets" that address the many different types of grief and loss children experience.

  Some popular series books are:

    - The *Sometimes Series*, (1-4) – includes six books that address ADHD, social problems, anger control, shyness, depression and anxiety

    - The *Early Prevention Series*, (2-4) – includes nine books that address topics such as negative thinking, shyness, responsibility and self-control

    - The *Learning to Get Along Series*, (K-3) – includes 14 books that each focus on a specific social skill – such as following rules, kindness, accepting others, personal safety and listening

Anger Management and Conflict Resolution

A second grader uses mean words on the playground, a kindergartener cheats on a board game, and a fifth grader realizes that a rumor is being spread about her. All of these situations can evoke strong feelings of anger in a child. This anger can manifest itself in a variety of ways – including physical altercations, verbal outbursts or complete withdrawal from a class activity. Counselors are frequently called upon to assist both teachers and students during and after these angry episodes.

The books in this section give children the opportunity to identify with characters that experience similar angry events. These stories give children permission to feel anger and a chance to explore their anger "triggers." Through the realistic storylines, children witness healthy (and unhealthy) coping strategies and are asked to internalize the strategies that might be effective for them. Above all, they learn that anger is a healthy emotion and that conflict resolution is an important life skill.

Josh's Smiley Faces

Book: *Josh's Smiley Faces: A Story About Anger* by Gina Ditta-Donahue

Publisher: Magination Press

Grade Levels: K-2

Setting: Individual, Group, Classroom

Book Description

Seven-year-old Josh gets in trouble at home because he has a hard time controlling his angry feelings. So his mom comes up with a fun and creative incentive program that rewards Josh every time he uses words to express his anger, instead of throwing or breaking things. It's not easy for Josh to change his behavior, but once he earns his first smiley face, he's hooked, and he starts to manage his anger. This is a great story to help children with anger problems understand that they are not alone. The book also includes a detailed outline of steps parents or teachers can take to implement an anger management program for their child(ren).

Materials Needed

- ***Introduction -*** *a red balloon (not inflated)*
- ***Extension Activity #1 -*** *5-10 magazines with lots of photos/advertisements of people*
- ***Extension Activity #2 -*** *a large, soft ball*

Preparation: None needed

Introduction

Invite students to the reading area and have them sit in a large circle. Tell students you're having a certain feeling today and you'd like them to guess what it is. Show students your angriest face – the more exaggerated the better. Ask students to think about something that makes them really angry and have them show you what their face looks like when they're really angry. After they've practiced their angry faces, ask them to show you what their body looks like when they're angry. Next, ask students to think about something that makes them feel happy, and have them show you what their faces and bodies look like when they feel this way. Ask students which feeling makes them feel more relaxed.

Tell students you're going to share a story with them about a little boy named Josh who has a hard time controlling his anger. Show students a deflated red balloon, and tell them that the balloon represents Josh's anger. Ask them to watch what happens to the balloon as you read the story. As you're reading the story, blow a little air into the balloon every time something happens to make Josh angry. At the end of the story ask students what would happen to the balloon if Josh kept letting his anger get worse? Ask students to name some things Josh could do to calm down and feel less angry. Each time a student names an anger management strategy, release a little bit of air from the balloon, until eventually the balloon is deflated and all the anger is gone.

Follow-up Questions (after reading)

1. What were some of the things that made Josh angry?

2. What did Josh's body and face look like when he was angry?

3. What did Josh's mom tell him to do when he was angry?

4. What did Josh have to do in order to earn smiley faces for his chart?

5. Was it easy or hard for Josh to control his anger? What are some things you can do/words you can use next time you're angry?

Extension Activities

1. Show students various magazine photos of people who are angry and ask them to point out the different facial and body clues that identify the anger. Help students draw parallels between themselves and the people in the photographs – do they show their anger the same way or a different way? Ask students to close their eyes for 20-30 seconds and imagine something happening to them that makes them feel very angry. When they open their eyes, ask students if any of their bodies gave them "anger clues," and allow them time to share the different anger clues they felt. Explain to students that being aware of how our face and body react when we're angry can help us recognize anger early so that we can keep it from getting worse.

2. Have students stand in a large circle. Tell them you'd like to play "angry ball" with them. Start the game off by completing the following sentence: "I feel angry when…" Ask for a volunteer who can repeat what you said. Toss the student the angry ball and ask him to repeat what you said and then complete the sentence using his own words. The student should then throw the ball to another student, who should repeat what was just said and then add her own sentence.

Activity with Reproducible

Have students brainstorm out loud some of the things that make them angry and things that make them happy. Give several students an opportunity to share with the class. Distribute the following activity sheet to students and tell them you'd like them to write or draw things that make them angry on the left side (under the angry face) and things that make them happy on the right side (under the happy face).

My Angry and Happy Feelings

Things that make me

ANGRY

Things that make me

HAPPY

_____

_____

_____

_____

_____

_____

_____

_____

Sometimes I'm Bombaloo

Book: *Sometimes I'm Bombaloo* by Rachel Vail

Publisher: Scholastic Paperbacks

Grade Levels: K-2

Setting: Individual, Group, Classroom

Book Description

Katie Honors describes herself as a good kid – most of the time. She gives wonderful hugs, shares her toys with her brother and remembers the "magic word" when she wants something. However, when she gets REALLY angry, she becomes a self-described Bombaloo, a monster that shows its anger through yelling, screaming and scrunching up its face. After having some quiet time in time-out, Katie calms down and realizes that being Bombaloo can be kind of scary. Through her mother's reassuring actions, Katie understands the importance of handling her anger in a healthy way. Written in kid-friendly language, this book offers many ways to explore angry feelings and practice healthy coping skills.

Materials Needed

- ***Extension Activity #1 -*** *PlayDoh®, bubbles, crayons, and drawing paper*
- ***Activity with Reproducible -*** *crayons, pencils*

Preparation

- ***Extension Activity #1 -*** *Set up the three anger management stations around the room.*

Introduction

Ask students to come to the reading area. Show the book cover and tell them you are going to read a book about a girl that turns into Bombaloo. Ask them if they have ever heard of Bombaloo. Tell them that it is their job to figure out what Bombaloo is by the end of the story.

Follow-up Questions (after reading)

1. What feeling does Katie have when she turns into Bombaloo? Does she have "big feelings" or "little feelings" when she is Bombaloo?

2. What do you think happened to make Katie feel like Bombaloo? (the book does not tell us)

3. Why do you think her mom told her to go to her room to have a time-out? Do you ever have time-outs when you are angry?

4. What makes you feel Bombaloo? What do you do when you feel this way?

Extension Activities

1. Explain to students that angry feelings live in our bodies. It is our job to get those angry feelings out of our bodies in a healthy way, in a way that does not hurt us or anyone else. Tell students that you are going to share three of your favorite strategies for releasing angry feelings. The students should rotate around the three stations, so they can experience each one.

   A. PlayDoh® Station
   Demonstrate rolling, punching and squeezing the PlayDoh® to release angry feelings.

   B. Bubbles Station
   Demonstrate deep, slow breaths in through the nose and out through the mouth. Show them that short, hard breaths break, rather than create, the bubbles.

   C. Scribble Stories Station
   Demonstrate scribbling on large pieces of drawing paper. Students should also be given the option of scrunching up their papers and throwing them in the trashcan after they are finished.

2. Building upon follow-up question #1, talk about "big feelings" versus "little feelings." Give them an example of something that makes you "little mad," such as someone bumping into you or not sharing their snack with you. Next, give them an example of something that makes you "big mad," such as someone calling you a mean name or not being honest. Use your arms to demonstrate the "big" and "little" feelings. Give students several different scenarios and ask them to show you whether they would have "big feelings" or "little feelings" about that situation. Point out that one situation can make two people feel very differently.

Activity with Reproducible

Ask students to think about the last time they were so angry that they felt like Bombaloo. Hand out the activity sheet and tell students to draw their Bombaloo story. Ask them to draw what was happening right before they turned into Bombaloo. Ask them to finish the writing prompt or assist them as needed.

My Bombaloo Story

Directions: *Think about a time when you were so angry that you turned into Bombaloo. Complete the sentence and draw a picture below.*

I turned into Bombaloo when ____________________

____

____

____

Name ____

The Butter Battle

Book: *The Butter Battle* by Dr. Seuss

Publisher: Random House Books for Young Readers

Grade Levels: 3-5

Setting: Small Group, Classroom

Book Description

The Yooks and the Zooks have been in a battle with each other for years over the correct way to butter their bread. As their conflict mounts, they develop more and more sophisticated weapons in an attempt to outdo each other and win the battle. This book has no true ending, which makes it a great discussion starter for healthy ways to deal with conflict. *Note: the word "bomb" is used in the book – this might be frightening for some children, and inappropriate in most classrooms. You can either read the book exactly as written and explain to children that it was written in a very different time period than we live in now, or you can choose to substitute a different word when reading.

Materials Needed

- ***Introduction -*** *several ambiguous pictures (those that can be seen two different ways – ex. old woman/ young woman, rabbit/duck)*
- ***Activity with Reproducible -*** *a hole punch and 4-6 brad fasteners*

Preparation

- ***Activity with Reproducible -*** *Copy enough wheels so each group of four has one. Cut the wheels out and fasten them with brads (you can choose to let the students do this but you'll need to allow extra time).*

Introduction

Ask students to raise their hands if they have ever had a problem or disagreement with a friend, parent, sibling, cousin, or teacher. Allow an opportunity for several students to share examples of arguments they've had with others. Engage students in a brief discussion by asking some of the following questions: Is it okay to disagree? Does every problem always have a solution, or a right or wrong answer? Is fighting with words better than fighting with our bodies? Are our arguments always over important things?

Show students your examples of ambiguous pictures. Make the point that everyone sees a situation from a different perspective. Explain to students that every story has at least two sides – yet often, when we are faced with a conflict, we are only able – or willing – to see our own side of the story. The person on the other side of the conflict is also only able to see his side. Ask students if they think any progress can be made this way. Help students understand that if neither side is willing to listen to the other side, and both sides are convinced they're right, the conflict will never be solved – it will only get worse. Yet when we are willing and able to listen to the other person's side, and to try and "put ourselves in their shoes," then we are on the right path to solving our conflict. By listening to the other point of view, we are also showing care and respect, and people will be more likely to listen to us. Tell children you'd like to share a book with them about a conflict that started over something small and silly but grew very big because it wasn't resolved the right way.

Follow-up Questions (after reading)

1. What was the conflict between the Yooks and the Zooks?

2. What did one of the Zooks do that set the butter battle into motion? What could he have done instead?

3. What were some of the crazy contraptions the Yooks and the Zooks came up with? Why do you think it was so important for them to build bigger and better machines? Is winning everything? Do you think they could have made other choices?

4. Why do you think the story didn't have a real ending? What do you think happened?

5. Do you think the Yooks and Zooks learned anything from the Butter Battle? How is the Butter Battle similar to things in our world today?

Extension Activities

1. Write a math problem on the board but intentionally leave out a number. For example 6 + ___ = ____. Ask students to raise their hand if they know the answer to the problem. Some students will likely raise their hands and guess an answer. Redirect students by explaining that there's no way to solve the math problem because we don't have all the information we need. Explain to students that this is also true for problems with people – we can't solve conflicts without all the information, and we can't get all the information unless we listen to the other person and try to understand her side. Tell students that in order to solve any problem, we need to have all the facts. Go back to the math problem and insert a number. Ask students if they know the answer since they now have more information. Help students understand that while a math problem usually only has one right answer, problems with people or situations often have several answers or solutions.

2. Stand in the middle of the room and tell students you'd like them to pretend that you represent conflict. Ask students to think about how they usually react when they experience a conflict themselves or see a conflict between others. Tell students you'd like them to put themselves – in relation to you – somewhere in the room that shows what their first response is to conflict and arguing. Ask them to think about the direction they're facing, (toward or away from the conflict) their distance from conflict (do they prefer to be close to it or far away) and the position their bodies are in. Stress to students that there is no right answer – it's very much an individual trait – and encourage them to make the decision for themselves, rather than following their friends. Once all students have found their position in the room, ask for individual volunteers to explain why they chose to stand where they are. Have students remain standing, and ask them to take turns completing the following sentence aloud: "When I get into a conflict, I usually …"

Activity with Reproducible

Discuss with students that there are many ways to resolve conflicts, and that you'd like to teach them some of the strategies you think are most helpful. Tell students that afterward, you will give them an opportunity to divide into groups and practice the strategies on their own. Review the following strategies with students (you may want to write these on the board or on a large piece of chart paper):

1) Talk it out – this is one of the most helpful strategies, because it allows both sides to share their story and be heard. When using this strategy, stress to students that it's very important they not interrupt each other.

2) Express your feelings – Let the other side know exactly how you feel about what happened, using an I-message: I feel _____ when you _____.

3) Flip a coin / Rock, paper, scissors, etc. – when trying to resolve a simple conflict, sometimes it's easiest and most helpful to leave it up to luck and chance.

4) Compromise/Make a Deal – this is when both sides "meet in the middle," so that everybody wins. Choosing to take turns is a good example of this.

5) Postpone – put off resolving the conflict until you have calmed down and are better able to think clearly.

6) Humor – sometimes, joking about the conflict helps lighten the mood enough to put things in perspective. Be sure to laugh at the situation, and not at the person.

7) Ignore – walking away from the conflict or just "shrugging it off" is best sometimes.

8) Get help – for especially difficult problems, or when other strategies don't work, it's a great idea to ask for help from a parent, teacher or trusted relative.

Divide students into groups of four and give each group a conflict resolution wheel (or have each group cut out their wheel and arrow and fasten it with a brad). If you have cut out the wheels ahead of time, make sure to give each group a copy of the 14 conflict scenarios. Tell students you'd like them to take turns choosing a conflict from the scenario list and then spin the conflict resolution wheel and think of a response to that particular conflict that uses the strategy they landed on. Allow students approximately 10-15 minutes to play the game. Afterward, give students time to share which strategies they felt would work the best, and which strategies they felt most comfortable using.

Conflict Resolution Wheel

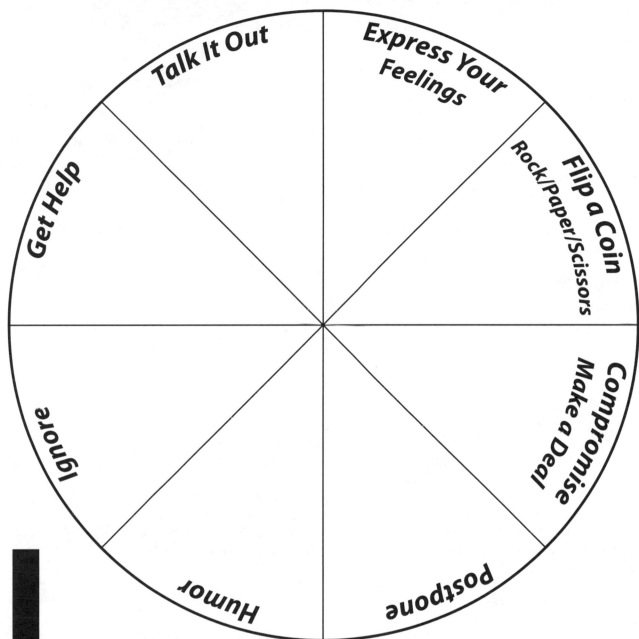

Talk It Out

Express Your Feelings

Get Help

Flip a Coin
Rock/Paper/Scissors

Ignore

Compromise
Make a Deal

Humor

Postpone

Conflict Scenarios

1. A classmate keeps taking your pencils.
2. You see someone copy your paper.
3. Another student always gossips about you.
4. Other students won't let you join their game.
5. Your friend borrowed a video game and lost it.
6. Someone trips you on purpose.
7. A classmate laughs at you every time you talk.
8. Someone calls you a mean name.
9. A classmate spread a cruel rumor about you.
10. A friend didn't invite you to his/her birthday party.
11. Your mom won't let you go to the movies/mall.
12. Your brother lost your favorite CD.
13. Someone makes fun of how you look.
14. A friend blames you for something you didn't do.

The Very Angry Day That Amy Didn't Have

Book: *The Very Angry Day That Amy Didn't Have* by Lawrence Shapiro

Publisher: Childswork/Childsplay

Grade Levels: 1-4

Setting: Individual, Small Group, Classroom

Book Description

Margaret and Amy are two girls in the same class who both happen to be having a bad day. While Amy is able to find ways to solve the many problems that arise, Margaret isn't able to handle her frustrations, and she gets angrier and angrier as the day goes on.

Materials Needed

- **Extension Activity #1 -** *marshmallows, toothpicks, large styrofoam ball*
- **Extension Activity #2 -** *paper bag*

Preparation: None needed

Introduction

Ask students to think about a time recently when they felt angry. Allow them a few minutes to share their stories. Ask the students who shared their stories if they stayed angry for a long time, or if their anger went away quickly. Ask them if there was anything that helped them deal with their anger. Discuss with students that anger itself is not a bad thing, but that sometimes people make bad choices when they are angry – like taking their anger out on others. Explain that sometimes when one thing goes wrong for us, everything after that goes wrong too –because we react to the first thing in an angry way, which sets our mood for the day. Tell students that today they will be talking about good choices to make when they are angry. Show students the cover of the book and have them guess what it may be about, taking clues from the title and the cover picture.

Follow-up Questions (after reading)

1. Did Margaret and Amy have the same kind of things happen to both of them during their day? Did they have the same mood about their day?

2. How did Margaret react to some of the things that happened to her? How did Amy react to some of the things that happened to her? Who chooses the way we react to problems we face?

3. What happened between Margaret and Billy? How did Amy feel when she saw this? What made her decide not to fight with Margaret about it?

4. What other things did Margaret do to people because she was mad?

5. How did Margaret feel when Amy told her how she didn't like the way she acted? Do you think Margaret's day will go differently next time she's angry? Why or why not?

6. When you are angry, does it ruin your whole day? Do you show your anger more like Margaret or more like Amy?

Extension Activities

1. Have students sit in a circle. Distribute several toothpicks to each student. Pass a Styrofoam ball around the circle. Ask each student to name one thing that makes them really angry and have them stick a toothpick in the ball as they speak. Go around the circle several times so all students have a chance to name several things that make them angry. Pass the ball around again and ask students how it feels to hold it (prickly, uncomfortable). Explain that this is how we feel when we keep anger inside of us and don't deal with it properly. Have students pass the ball around again, this time naming one positive way they can handle their anger. This time, have students put a marshmallow on each toothpick as they speak. Once the toothpicks have all been covered, pass the ball around again. Talk about how much better it feels when we have dealt with our angry feelings and resolved our anger.

2. Blow up a paper bag and, once it's totally full of air, pop it suddenly, to demonstrate exploding. Explain to students that this is what happens when we let anger build up and don't deal with it in healthy ways. Talk about alternative ways that students can deal with their anger – breathing deeply, counting to 10, talking to a friend or parent about what made them angry, running or jumping rope, playing ball, etc. Have students brainstorm as many ideas as possible and write them on a white board or chart paper.

Activity with Reproducible

Show students pictures or photographs of rivers and lakes. Ask students to think about what happens to the water when they throw a rock into a lake or pond (it sends ripples across the water's surface). Explain that anger can have a "ripple effect" too, if we don't handle it the right way. Review the ripples that Margaret caused in the story. Help students understand how our anger can be just like the rock thrown in the water – it makes a big splash and then spreads to other people. Ask students to think about the following example: You get angry and shout at your mom, then your mom is upset with you for yelling at her, and so your mom gets mad at your sister for doing something that usually wouldn't make her mad. Then your sister is in a bad mood because she got in trouble….explain to students how quickly the ripple effect can reach many different people. Tell students you'd like them to think about something in their life that they've gotten mad about – or are currently mad about – and then think about the different "ripples" the anger can cause. Ask them to complete the following activity sheet and give students time to share at the end.

My Anger Ripples

Directions: *Think of something that has made you angry recently, and write this inside the bullseye (target). Next, think about the different "ripples" your anger caused – and write each ripple in the designated circle, starting with ripple #1.*

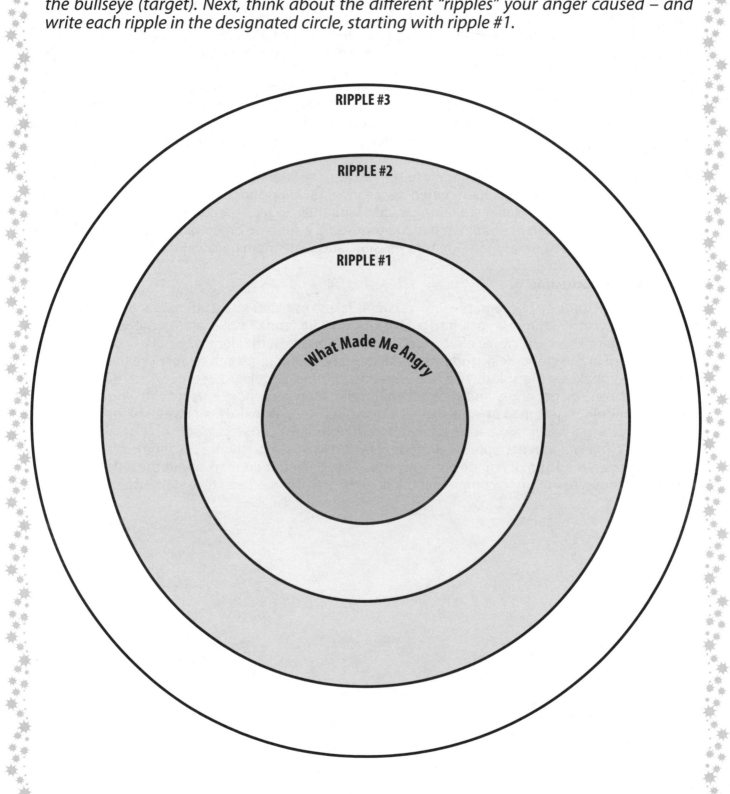

RIPPLE #3

RIPPLE #2

RIPPLE #1

What Made Me Angry

© YouthLight, Inc.

Anxiety and Worrying

A worried child is an anxious child. Whether the fears are based on realistic or unrealistic events, being scared is a powerful experience. Teachers, parents and counselors alike witness children using various coping skills to combat their worries. However, when children are unable to access or utilize healthy coping skills, they are at risk of shutting down or withdrawing from activities.

The books in this section introduce children to characters that experience worries similar to their own. Children are reassured that they *do* have control over their worries, and they are exposed to healthy and practical strategies for handling both big and little worries. The books and lessons in this section are appropriate for children who are infrequent worriers as well as those that worry constantly.

Is a Worry Worrying You?

Book: *Is a Worry Worrying You?* by Ferida Wolff and Harriet May Savitz

Publisher: Tanglewood Press

Grade Levels: K-3

Setting: Individual, Group, Classroom

Book Description

What is a worry? Is it a monster hiding under your bed? Is it a playground bully? Is it a scary new teacher on the first day of school? Through realistic scenarios, the author leads readers through a story about common childhood fears. Children learn creative problem-solving strategies and ways to "pack up their worries in suitcases and send them away." This is a wonderful book for students with a vivid imagination. It's an appropriate book for chronic and occasional worriers alike.

Materials Needed

- ***Introduction -*** *large, smooth rock (available at craft stores)*
- ***Extension Activity #1 and #2 -*** *crayons/markers, chart paper*
- ***Extension Activity #3 -*** *drawing paper, paint (finger paint is preferable)*
- ***Activity with Reproducible -*** *large mailing envelopes, helium balloon*

Preparation: None needed

Introduction

Invite students to come to the reading area. Show them a large, smooth rock and ask them to identify its identity. Explain that it is not just any old rock, but rather a special rock. It is your worry rock. Ask them if they have ever heard of a worry. Collect answers. Explain that whenever you (the counselor) are worried, you bring out your worry rock and rub it until your worry goes away. Tell students that you will be reading a book about worries because being worried is a very common feeling.

Follow-up Questions (after reading)

1. In the story, the illustrator drew a monster on each page. What do you think the monster represented in the story? Do you agree that worries can sometimes feel like monsters?

2. What were the little boy and girl's worries in the story? How did they handle their worries?

3. Do you ever have worries? What do you worry about?

4. How does your body feel when you are worried? How do you get rid of your worries?

5. Who helps you when you are feeling worried? What do they do to make your worries go away?

Extension Activities

1. On a large sheet of chart paper, ask students to recall the different strategies that the book offered to get rid of worries. Some of these strategies include hiding the worry in a closet, playing cards and baking a cake. After the students list the strategies from the book, ask them if they think they can come up with 10-20 additional (fun) things to do instead of worrying. Title the list, "_____Things to do Instead of Worrying!" Hang it in the room for children to reference throughout the year.

2. Give students an opportunity to practice reframing their thoughts through this "no worry" activity. Create a list of 5-10 things that an early childhood student might worry about throughout their day. Ask them to think of a more positive way to think about the worry. For example, the worry might be, "What if I do not get to be partners with my best friend in gym class?' The "no worry" thought could be, "Maybe I'll make a new friend in PE if I do not get matched up with my best friend." Allow students to act out the "worry and no worry" thoughts.

3. In the book, the worry was depicted as a monster. Ask students to draw/create their own version of a worry monster. Use markers, crayons or paint if available (finger paint would be ideal).

Activity with Reproducible

In the book, the author suggests putting the worry in a suitcase or envelope and sending it away. Allow students to practice this strategy by giving them a copy of the activity sheet and asking them to draw one of their biggest worries. After they finish their worry pictures, give them an opportunity to share their drawings with the group. It is important to make this an optional activity. Next, ask them to fold their papers as many times as they like. Provide a large mailing envelope for them to deposit their drawings. Ask them to choose a place where they would like to mail their worries. After deciding the destination as a group, tell them that you will mail their worries so that they do not have to worry about them anymore. If you can arrange to mail them to friend or colleague, ask them to write a letter to the students, explaining that they got the letter and looked at all of their worries. **If you are doing this with an individual student, you can have them write or draw their worry on a helium balloon. Go outside and have them release their balloon into the air as they say farewell to their worry.

I'm mailing my worry away....

Name _____

Something Might Happen

Book: *Something Might Happen* by Helen Lester

Publisher: Houghton Mifflin Books for Children

Grade Levels: K-3

Setting: Individual, Small Group, Classroom

Book Description

Twitchly Fidget is a lemur who's afraid to do absolutely anything because of what he fears might happen. In Twitchly's imagination, every opportunity poses the threat of disaster. So he sits alone in his dreary, windowless, doorless hut and worries. Then one day something *does* happen: Twitchly's Aunt Bridget Fidget drops in for a visit, and she can see right away that Twitchly needs "a fixin!" But will Aunt Bridget be able to persuade Twitchly to confront his fears?

Materials Needed

- ***Extension Activity #1*** - *stacks of old magazines, glue, and one small 8 x 8 square of poster board per student*
- ***Extension Activity #2*** - *drawing paper*

Preparation

- ***Extension Activity #1*** - *Cut out one 8 x 8 square of poster board for every student.*

Introduction

Ask students to raise their hands if they've ever felt afraid of something. Give students several minutes to discuss what some of their fears were, and give them an opportunity to express *why* they had the fears they did. Ask the students who shared their fears if they still have the same fears, or if someone or something helped them get over their fear. Try to draw comparisons between the different fears students share, if possible. Explain to students that often we're afraid of things because they are new and different, and we don't know what to expect. Help students understand that sometimes there's no good reason to be afraid of something, and that sometimes our fears prevent us from being able to enjoy things in life. Tell students that you are going to read them a book about a lemur who is scared of absolutely everything, and ask them to listen for times in the story when they have felt the same way as Twitchly.

Follow-up Questions (after reading)

1. What were some of the things Twitchly was afraid of?

2. Why was he afraid of these things? What did he think would happen?

3. How do you think his friends felt when they kept asking Twitchly to do things with them and he wouldn't?

4. Who helped Twitchly with his fears? How did she help? Who helps you with your fears?

5. What happened to Twitchly when he faced each of his fears?

6. Do you think Twitchly will be afraid of things anymore? What lesson do you think he learned?

Extension Activities

1. Discuss with students how our fears can keep us from exploring the world and doing what we really want to do. Point out how much Twitchly missed out on by being too afraid to try things. Divide students into groups of three or four, and give each a group a stack of old magazines, a small square of poster board and some glue. Have students go through the magazine and tear out pictures of things that make them anxious or afraid. Ask students to glue these images onto their poster board square to form a "fear collage." When all students have finished, allow them an opportunity to share their collages with the class.

2. Talk with students about how Aunt Bridget Fidget helped Twitchly face his fears and overcome them. Ask students to name some people in their lives who help them when they're afraid. Once children have named people who help them, ask if any of them are comforted by a special place or object. Give each child a piece of drawing paper and ask them to draw a line down the middle. On one side they should draw a picture – with accompanying words – of something that makes them afraid or worried. On the other side, tell students you'd like them to draw a picture of a person, place or object that helps them feel less afraid or worried.

Activity with Reproducible

Ask students to think of a baby taking its first steps. Does a baby automatically walk perfectly with the first step? Explain to children that sometimes we have to take baby steps to help us get over our fears. Sometimes it's impossible to get over our fears all at once, but if we take one small step at a time, it's a lot easier. Distribute the activity sheet to students and tell them that you'd like them to write their fear on the line at the top and that in each of the footprints, you'd like them to write and draw the different steps they're going to take to overcome their fear.

Facing My Fear...
One Step at a Time

Directions: Write your fear on the line at the top of the paper, and in each of the footprints, write and draw the different steps you are going to take to get over your fear.

_____

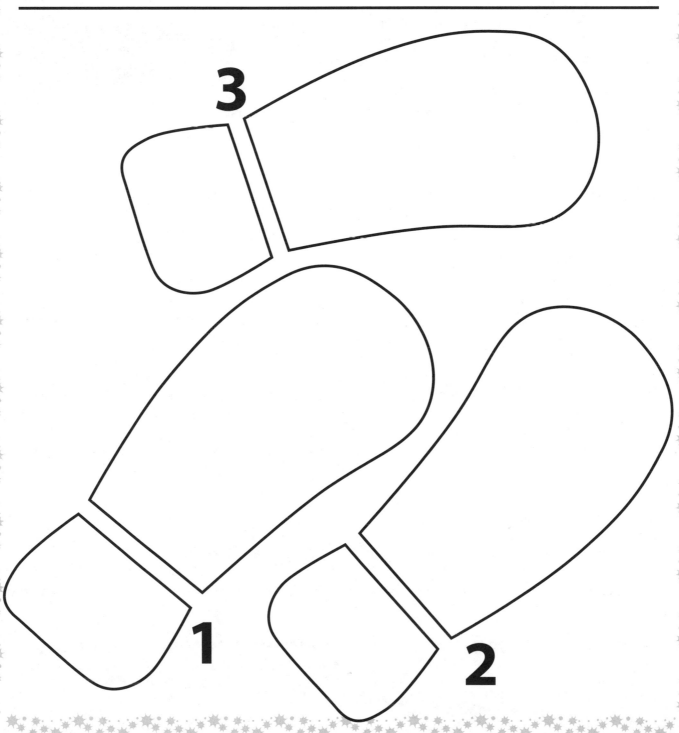

The Kissing Hand

Book: *The Kissing Hand* by Audrey Penn

Publisher: Tanglewood Press

Grade Levels: K-2

Setting: Individual, Group, Classroom

Book Description

Chester, the raccoon, is very nervous about his very first day at school. He thinks it would be much more fun to stay at home with his mother in his familiar surroundings. Through her encouraging words and reassuring actions, his mom convinces him to be brave and optimistic about his new adventure. Additionally, she gives him a kiss on the palm of his hand and instructs him to hold his "Kissing Hand" up by his face when he feels sad or lonely throughout the day. This is a wonderful book to read on the first day of school or with a child separated from her parents for various reasons.

Materials Needed

- *Introduction -* raccoon puppet
- *Extension Activity #1 -* heart stamp or heart stickers
- *Extension Activity #2 -* sign language book
- *Activity with Reproducible -* crayons

Preparation

- *Extension Activity #2 -* Locate sign language resources, either in books or on online, and identify several signs to teach to the students.

Introduction

Invite students to the reading area. Introduce them to your friend, Chester. Ask them if they have ever seen an animal like this. Do they know any special facts about raccoons? Explain that one of the unique qualities about raccoons is that they sleep during the day and are awake at night. This is called nocturnal. Tell them that Chester wanted to visit their classroom so badly that he stayed awake all day just so that he could join them. He wants to pass on a special gift that his mother gave him. They will need to listen to the story to find out the identity of the special gift.

Follow-up Questions (after reading)

1. How was Chester feeling at the beginning of the story?

2. What was the special secret his mother passed onto him? What were her instructions about using the special gift?

3. Have you ever been scared to do something new? How did you make yourself feel better?

4. Do you think Chester enjoyed his first day of school? Do you think he was still a bit nervous at different points throughout the day?

5. How can you help other students when they feel lonely or scared?

Extension Activities

1. Give all students their own Kissing Hand by placing a heart stamp or heart sticker on their hand (either in their palm or on the back of their hand). This is to remind them they are loved by many people, including their family and friends. If they feel sad or lonely throughout the day, they can place their kissing hand close to their face as their reminder.

2. The sign for "I love you" is illustrated on the last page of the book. Teach students several other signs, such as *please, thank you* and *friend*, that they can use in the classroom with their friends. There are many books and websites, such as www.lifeprint.com, that can help you.

Activity with Reproducible

Explain to students that another strategy for getting rid of the "worries," is to think of a special place that makes you feel warm, cozy and safe. Maybe it is your bedroom or the beach? Maybe it is your backyard or a comfortable chair at home? Perhaps it is sitting on your grandma's lap or taking a nap in your bed? Distribute the activity sheet and crayons and ask students to draw a picture of their special place. Invite them to share their drawings with you or the class. Allow students to keep the picture in their desk or locker so they can reference it when they are feeling anxious or lonely.

My Special Place

Directions: *Think of a place that makes you feel warm, safe and cozy. Maybe it is your bedroom? Maybe it is under an old tree in your backyard? Maybe it is beside your pet? Draw a picture of your special place. Be sure to include details of this place, such as the color of the walls or the objects around you.*

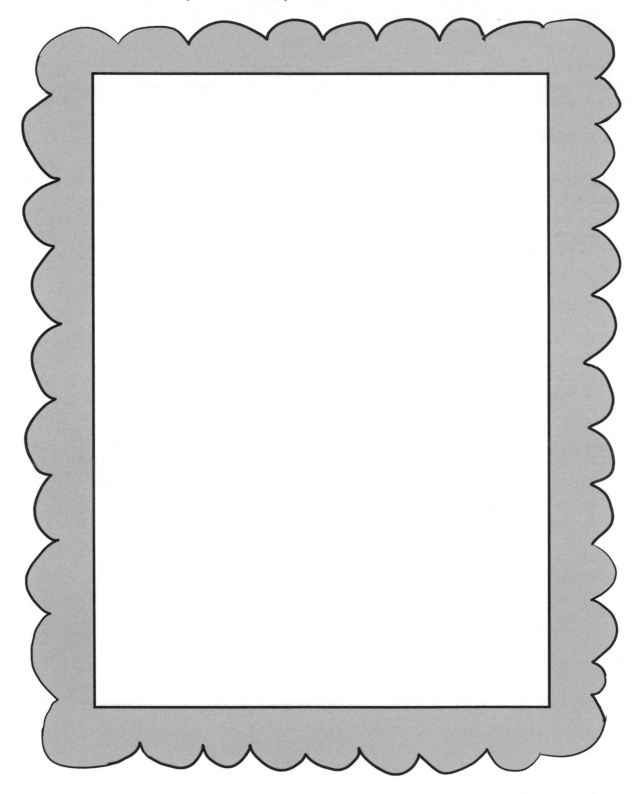

© YouthLight, Inc.

Wemberly Worried

Book: *Wemberly Worried* by Kevin Henkes

Publisher: Greenwillow Books

Grade Levels: 1-3

Setting: Individual, Small Group, Classroom

Book Description

Wemberly the mouse worries about absolutely everything – from trees falling on her house to creatures in the radiator. On the first day of school, she meets someone who worries just as much as Wemberly does. The two form a fast friendship, and learn an important lesson about courage along the way.

Materials Needed

- ***Introduction -*** *small container of rocks or pebbles, bathroom scale*
- ***Extension Activity #1 -*** *a flat rock or stone for every child*
- ***Extension Activity #2 -*** *slips of paper, a stuffed animal to leave in the classroom, and an empty tissue box*

Preparation: None needed

Introduction

Have students come to the reading area. Ask students to raise their hands if they have ever worried about anything? Lead them into a short discussion of the various components of worry – How do our bodies feel when we are worried? What are some things children worry about? How else can worries affect us? What do you think are some good ways to handle worry?

Bring in a container of small to medium sized rocks or pebbles. Ask for a volunteer to come to the front of the room and put as many rocks as possible into his/her pockets. Ask the student how they feel with all the rocks in their pockets – is it easier or harder to walk? To sit down? To run? Have the student get on the scale and then record their weight on the board. Ask the class how much they think the rocks weighed – and then have the student remove the rocks and weigh him/her again, recording the weight. Explain to students that our worries are like rocks weighing us down and keeping us from being able to do what we want to do.

Follow-up Questions (after reading)

1. What were some of the things Wemberly worried about?

2. What advice did Wemberly's parents give her? Do your parents give you advice when you worry?

3. What was Wemberly's newest worry in the story?

4. What happened when she went to her first day of school? How did you feel on your very first day of school?

5. How do you think Wemberly felt at the end of the book? What did she learn?

Extension Activities

1. Give each student in the class one rock or stone – the stones should be large enough to write on, but not large enough to hurt anyone. Tell students that this is their worry stone, and you would like them to write one worry (more if they have room) they have on the stone. Students may draw a picture or symbol of their worry instead, if they wish. When all students are finished, have them put their worry stone in their pocket and take them to an appropriate area outside, where they can throw their worry away. You may choose to have them throw the worry in a large trashcan outside, or in an open field or wooded area near the school. When students have thrown their worries away, lead students in a deep breathing exercise to help them relax, and completely let go of their worry.

2. What helped Wemberly's worry go away was meeting a friend she had something in common with and could share things with. Ask each student to write down one worry they have on a slip of paper, and have them write their name at the top. After you've collected all the worries, go through them and match students up according to common worries they may have. Tell students this will be their "listening buddy" for the year, and encourage them to talk to their buddy whenever they have a worry about something. Give them a few minutes to share their worries with each other now, and then designate a meeting place in the classroom where they can go throughout the year to share their worries. Or, instead of matching students up, introduce a stuffed animal that can be left in the classroom for students to share their worries with – a "Furry Worry." Have the animal set up in a designated area of the classroom along with some slips of paper and pencils and a "worry box." Encourage students to write down any worries they may have and drop them in the worry box – they can address their worries to the "Furry Worry." Each time you go in the classroom throughout the year, take a few minutes to pull some worries from the worry box and talk through the worries with students.

Activity with Reproducible

Ask students to show you what their faces and bodies look like when they are worried. Point out to students that Wemberly felt less worried about everything once she met a friend who she had something in common with, and once she started to feel more comfortable at school. Tell students you'd like them to think about the people, places and things that might help them feel better when they are worried. Allow time for students to share examples. Distribute the following worksheet to students and read each of the four squares aloud to them. Ask students to fill in each of the four squares by drawing and writing the answer to the question.

All About My Worries...

Directions: In each of the four squares, draw a picture that shows how you feel or what you can do in that situation. After drawing your four pictures, use words to describe the pictures.

This is how I look when I'm worried:	**One thing I can do when I'm worried:**
When I am worried, I will talk to:	**One place I can go when I'm worried is:**

Bullying and Relational Aggression

Unfortunately, bullying is a problem that infiltrates classrooms around the country. It negatively affects students' self-esteem, which in turn, affects academic performance. Bullies are feared, victims are targeted, and bystanders are left feeling helpless. As a result, teachers, counselors and parents are called upon to support and educate their students so the cycle ends and healing begins.

The recently-coined term *relational aggression* gave a name to a unique form of bullying that is often used by girls. This type of bullying, which uses friendships as leverage, is typically done "below the radar screen," making it very difficult for adults to detect and intervene. However, the effects of relational aggression are devastating and long-lasting if not addressed appropriately.

Books are a powerful means to invite dialogue on this sensitive topic. While it is important for children to be able to relate to the characters in the stories, it is also equally important for the storylines to be realistic and believable. The following authors have created strong characters that utilize positive problem-solving strategies, which will ideally empower and inspire students to adopt similar strategies.

Just Kidding

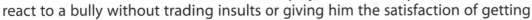

Book: *Just Kidding* by Trudy Ludwig

Publisher: Tricycle Press

Grade Levels: 2-5

Setting: Individual, Group, Classroom

Book Description

DJ has a big problem at school. His problem is his classmate, Vince. Whether it is picking basketball teams at recess or riding home on the school bus, Vince never misses an opportunity to send a put-down DJ's way. Vince's insincere phrase, "I was just kidding," makes DJ feel even worse. During a heart-to-heart conversation, DJ's dad helps him understand that kids who tease others typically have a lot of internal turmoil. His dad also role-plays different ways to react to a bully without trading insults or giving him the satisfaction of getting angry. DJ puts his new plan into action the next day and finds that it works, but only temporarily. As a result, DJ and his dad decide to go see the teacher to report the situation. She reassures him that reporting is much different than tattling. In the end, DJ discovers a group of friends that are able to joke around with one another without making fun of each other. Although all of the characters are male, the book is well-suited for girls, too.

Materials Needed

- ***Extension Activity #2 -*** *"Simon's Hook" by Karen Gedig Burnett*
- ***Extension Activity #3 -*** *large chart paper, markers*

Preparation: None

Introduction

Ask students to raise their hands if they enjoy watching funny movies and TV shows. Ask them to explain why they enjoy watching these types of programs. Talk about the importance of humor in making us feel good. Explain that humor can also make people feel badly if it is directed at them in a mean way. Introduce the book and tell students they are going to hear a story about teasing and humor that crossed the line and turned into bullying.

Follow-up Questions (after reading)

1. How does Vince make DJ feel like a "loser?"

2. What do you think about DJ's dad's advice? What did you notice about the way his dad approached DJ when he was angry?

3. How do you think Vince really felt about DJ? Give some evidence to support your answer.

4. Do you agree with the teacher's definition of tattling versus reporting? Was there ever a time that you were scared to report something to a teacher?

5. Have you ever been in a situation where teasing "crossed the line?" Were you the giver or receiver of the teasing?

Extension Activities

1. In the story, DJ's dad and brother play a game with DJ, practicing anti-teasing stragegies. These strategies include agreeing with the teaser and using humor to diffuse the situation. The only rule of the game is that he can't say or do anything mean back to the teaser. Allow students to play a similar game by pairing up the students and asking them to come up with a teasing sentence. They also need to create a response that follows the "no teasing" rules. For example, one student might say, "Hey, loser!" The other student could say in response, "You are right, I lose my socks all the time!" Ask each pair to role play the teasing sentence and "no teasing" response.

2. As a follow-up story, read *Simon's Hook* by Karen Gedig Burnett. This book teaches similar concepts by illustrating different ways to "not take the bait."

3. Read the "Teasing Do's and Don'ts" at the end of book and discuss them as a class. Emphasize that humor has an important place in the classroom, but not at the expense of others. Using this page as a guide, create a Teasing Bill of Rights for the classroom. Write it on large chart paper and ask every student to sign it. Hang it in a prominent spot in the classroom.

Activity with Reproducible

Allow students to work in pairs to complete the *Just Kidding* crossword puzzle.

Answer Key:

DOWN	ACROSS
1. Reporting	3. Carefully
2. Body	4. Kidding
3. Counselor	6. Humor
5. Ignore	8. Respect
7. Upset	

Just Kidding!

Across

3. Use humor gently and _____.

4. Vince's famous line was "I am just_____!"

6. You can use this with a bully to diffuse the situation.

8. If someone asks you to stop teasing them, you need to _____ their feelings.

Down

1. Telling an adult when you or someone is in danger.

2. _____ language gives you important clues about someone's feelings.

3. DJ's teacher suggested that Vince may need to meet with the school _____.

5. DJ's dad taught him to _____ the bully.

7. DJ said that Vince made him feel this way.

My Secret Bully

Book: *My Secret Bully* by Trudy Ludwig

Publisher: Tricycle Press

Grade Levels: 3-5

Setting: Individual, Girls' Group

Book Description

Katie and Monica have been good friends since kindergarten. However, Monica is discouraged when Katie's friendship becomes inconsistent. Katie is nice to Monica when they are alone, but when they are at school, she makes mean comments and excludes her. Monica receives good advice from her mom about standing up to a bully. This is one of the few books that addresses female relational aggression.

Materials Needed

- *Extension Activity #2 - lined paper, pencils*
- *Activity with Reproducible - pencils*

Preparation: None needed

Introduction

Introduce the words *relational aggression* to the group or individual. Ask them if they are familiar with the words. Gather responses. If they are unfamiliar with the term, ask them what types of friendship problems girls their age typically experience. Answers will most likely include exclusion, rumors and backstabbing. Explain that these behaviors are all part of relational aggression, a form of emotional bullying that uses friendships as a way to attack one another. In this story, they will hear about relational bullying between two longtime friends.

Follow-up Questions (after reading)

1. Who was the bully in the story? Who was the victim? Who was the bystander?

2. How do you think the Katie (the bully) was feeling in the story?

3. Are girls the only ones who use relational aggression when they are angry? How do boys typically handle their anger?

4. Which character do you identify with in the story? Explain.

5. In the story, Monica goes to her mom for advice. Who do you go to for friendship advice?

Extension Activities

1. In the story, Monica learned to be assertive with her friend, Katie. Lead a short discussion about the difference between being assertive and being aggressive. Talk about the body language of an assertive person versus the body language of an aggressive person. Also, talk about the different motives of each person. An assertive individual's goal is to get their point across in a serious manner. An aggressive person's motive is to intimidate and provoke the other person. Do several role plays that demonstrate both types of behavior.

2. Building on follow-up question #5, hold a group "Dear Abby" talk show, where the girls get to be the friendship experts. Explain to the girls that "Dear Abby" is an advice column in the newspaper where people can submit their questions to an expert. First, ask students to (anonymously) write about one recent friendship problem they experienced on a piece of paper. In order to protect everyone's privacy, it is important to clarify that they should not use specific names in their letters. Collect the papers and read the questions to the group. Rotate "experts" so that each girl has an opportunity to answer one of the letters and give advice to the writer.

Activity with Reproducible

Using the reproducible, ask students to write a personal letter to either the bully, (Katie) victim, (Monica) or bystander in the story. Ask them to consider the following questions as they write the letter:

A) What advice do you want to give to the character?

B) Have you ever been in a similar situation?

C) What challenge do you have for her?

"Just Between Us Girls..."

Directions: *Write a personal letter to Katie, (the bully) Monica, (the victim) or one of the bystanders (you can make up a name for the bystander). Consider the following questions as you write the letter:*

1) What advice would you give to her?

2) Have you ever been in a similar situation? How did you handle it?

3) What challenge do you have for her?

Dear _____,

_____

_____

_____

_____

_____

_____

_____

_____

_____

Sincerely,

_____

Nobody Knew What to Do

Book: *Nobody Knew What to Do* by Becky Ray McCain

Publisher: Albert Whitman & Company

Grade Levels: 3-5

Setting: Individual, Small Group, Classroom

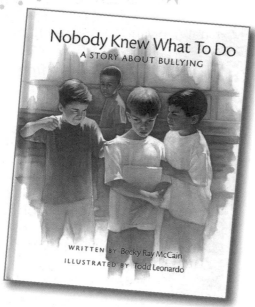

Book Description

When bullies pick on Ray at school, his classmates feel scared and confused, but "nobody knew what to do," and so they just stand by helplessly. Finally, after the bullying goes too far, one child finally finds the courage to tell his teacher about Ray. The students then invite Ray to join in their group, and with adult help, they are able to all stand up to the bullies.

Materials Needed

- *Extension Activity #1* - *a picture or photograph of a stop sign (or a school patrol stop sign if you have access to one)*
- *Extension Activity #2* - *one long sheet of white or beige chart paper, scotch tape*
- *Activity with Reproducible* - *basket or large cup*

Preparation

- *Extension Activity #2* - *Make a life-sized outline of a child that is non gender specific, draw a face on it, and cut it out.*
- *Activity with reproducible* - *Cut out the scenarios ahead of time and place them in a basket or large cup for students to draw from.*

Introduction

Have students gather around in a circle on the floor. Go around the circle and ask students what they think it means to be a bully. Ask students how many of them have ever known a bully. Ask students to raise their hand if they have ever been bullied, or if they've seen someone else bullied. Be sure to emphasize with students that bullying comes in several forms – physical, verbal and social/emotional, and make sure they understand they are all equally hurtful. Discuss the following questions with students: Why do certain students get bullied? Why do bullies do what they do? How can you keep from being bullied? What can you do when you see other students being bullied? Ask students to share examples from their lives, if any are comfortable doing so. Share the cover of the book with students and ask if they can guess why the book has the title it does.

Follow-up Questions (after reading)

1. Why do you think the students stood by and let Ray get bullied? What are some of the things the other students did to make it easier for them to watch Ray being bullied?

2. Did the bullies just bully Ray or did they bully everyone?

3. What made the book narrator finally decide to do something about the bullying? What two things did he do? Do you think it was easy or hard for the narrator to do these things?

4. What happened when the bullies came around again on the playground?

5. What lesson did you learn from this book?

Extension Activities

1. Show students a picture or photograph of a stop sign. Ask students if they have any ideas for how to STOP bullying. Allow students several minutes to share their ideas and suggestions. Then share with students the following 8 strategies for stopping a bully (one strategy for every corner of the stop sign). 1) Ignore it or walk away, 2) Be strong and brave – stand tall, speak clearly, make eye contact, 3) Use a firm voice to tell the person to stop, 4) Use an "I" message: "I feel _____ when you _____ because _____. I need you to _____. 5) Get help from an adult, 6) Help others who are being bullied, 7) Include everyone, 8) Do not bully others just because you are angry with them.

2. Put your life-sized cutout student on the board and tell students you'd like them to meet their new "classmate," Jack. Ask the students to pretend that Jack has just joined their class, but nobody is happy to have him here because everybody already has their own friends and nobody wants to share friends, or meet anyone new. Ask the students to take turns making fun of Jack and saying mean things to him. Every time a mean thing is said to Jack, tear off a large piece of Jack's body and hand it to the student who made the comment. Once everyone has had a chance to say something mean to Jack, have students come up, one at a time, and reattach their piece of Jack in the correct place. As each piece is reattached, the student must apologize to Jack for the mean thing that was said. When all students have reattached their piece of Jack, and apologized, ask students how they think Jack looks now. Students will likely say that he doesn't look very good, or that he doesn't look at all the same. Ask questions to help students understand that although they "fixed" some of the damage they caused, Jack is much worse than he was before, and he will never be exactly the same as before, because he was hurt so badly. Explain to students that when we hurt people with our words, we leave scars on them that will never go away. Hang Jack on a wall in the classroom to remind students of the power words have to hurt. (*Adapted from Gabrielle Ferry, M.A.*)

Activity with Reproducible

Review with students what happened in the story when the narrator finally decided to do something about the bullying of Ray. Reiterate to students that it is just as important for them to stand up for others who are being bullied as it is for them to stand up for themselves when they are being bullied. Emphasize to students that they each have the power to make a difference in the lives of others and to take a stand with bullies. Tell students you'd like to give them an opportunity to practice dealing with bullies by asking them to role play the following scenarios. Depending on the size and maturity of your group, you can choose to either have students come up individually to draw a scenario and tell how they would respond, or you can divide students into small groups and have them role play the scenarios together.

Role Play Scenarios

You have become good friends with the new girl in class. Your best friend is mad about this and says she won't be your friend anymore unless you stop talking to the new girl. What can you do?

Every day at recess, the same group of kids plays ball together. When you ask if you can join in and play, they say, "no way – we want to win, not lose! You can't even catch the ball." What can you do?

For the past three days, as you and a friend have been walking home from school, a group of boys from your grade has followed behind you and tried to trip your friend as he walks. What can you do?

You walk up to a group of your classmates at lunch and ask if you can sit with them. They all look at you and start laughing, then several of them get up and move to another table. What can you do?

One student in class always makes fun of another student's answers, ideas and projects. Today, when the teacher wasn't looking, the student looked at you and made the "loser" sign with his hands, then pointed to the first student. What can you do?

As you sit down at the lunch table, you overhear the other students at your table talking about you and whispering things to each other while looking your way. What can you do?

As you walk into the bathroom one day, you hear a group of girls in your class who are talking about another girl. They are making fun of what she looks like, laughing about her clothes, and calling her a loser. The girl they are talking about is your best friend. What can you do?

At lunch, your teacher has made a rule that there can only be 5 girls/boys at a table. Every day, the same 5 girls/boys scramble to sit together, and the new girl in your class is always the one left out. What can you do?

Every day in the cafeteria, there is one student from your class that sits alone. Other kids in your class always laugh at this student and whisper about him/her. What can you do?

A "friend" keeps asking you if he can copy the answers to your homework. You tell him no, but he keeps asking you every day, and he threatens to stop being your friend if you don't give him the answers. What can you do?

The Bully Blocker's Club

Book : *The Bully Blocker's Club* by Teresa Bateman

Publisher: Albert Whitman & Company

Grade Levels: 2-5

Setting: Individual, Small Group, Classroom

Book Description

Grant Grizzly is a bully who constantly taunts and teases Lotty Raccoon. After trying several different ways to deal with the bullying, Lottie finally decides to start a Bully Blockers Club. She recruits other students who have been bullied by Grant, and they come up with a clever solution for attracting the attention of adults and other students when they are being bullied.

Materials Needed

- *Introduction - two candles and something to light them with*
- *Extension Activity #1 - chart paper, markers and tape*
- *Extension Activity #2 - a handful of pencils (8-12)*

Preparation: None needed

Introduction

Ask students to raise their hand if they have ever been bullied, or if they have ever seen someone else bullied. Ask students why they think bullies choose to bully others, and if they have any ideas for stopping bullies. Encourage several students to share their stories, and after they have shared, ask the class if they noticed any similarities between the bullies in the shared stories. Explain to students that people are like candles – each one of us has the ability to bring light, warmth and happiness into the world. Yet sometimes a person or a group of people tries to make their flame bigger and brighter by putting out the flame of others. Show students how this never works - demonstrate by lighting two candles and blowing out one – the other is no brighter. Help students understand that when we help and include others, both people's flames will burn brighter. Relight the candle and put both flames together – the flames will join and both will shoot up taller and bigger flames. Reiterate that a bully tries to put out others' flames and tear them down – both physically and mentally, but we can choose to be a better person by standing up for what is right and helping others who are bullied. Tell students you'd like to share a book with them about some students who found a creative way to stop a bully.

Follow-up Questions (after reading)

1. What happened to Lotty at school every day? What were the different ways Grant bullied Lotty? Have you seen students at our school bully each other this way?

2. What was some of the advice Lotty's brother and sister gave? Did it work? Why not?

3. What did Lotty's teacher tell her? Did her suggestion help?

4. What did Lotty notice about Grant that helped her come up with the idea for the Bully Blocker's Club?

5. How did Lotty and her friends stand up to Grant for the first time? What happened when they did it? How do you think Lotty and her friends felt?

6. What did the kids in the Bully Blocker's Club do to help each other out? How did things change in Lotty's school as a result of the club?

Extension Activities

1. Divide students into teams of three or four and give each team a piece of chart paper and several markers. Ask students to work together to brainstorm suggestions for how to deal with a bully, and have them write their suggestions on chart paper. Make sure to emphasize that there are three different types of bullying – physical, verbal and social. When all the groups are finished (allow them approximately 10 minutes) temporarily tape the completed chart papers to the wall so students can view all the responses. Ask students if the same strategies came up in all the groups. Circle the three or four most common strategies and have different students volunteer to role play the strategies, using the following scenarios.

   - For the last two weeks, a student has been making fun of the way you run in P.E.

   - A student in your class puts her foot out to trip you every time you walk by her desk.

   - A student on the playground tells the other kids not to let you play with them. He pushes you away when you try to join a kickball game.

   - For the past week, the student who sits next to you has been taking your pencils out of your desk and then pretends like she hasn't taken them.

   - A student says that if you play with Sarah, she won't be your friend anymore.

   - Your classmate, George, makes fun of you every time you talk.

   - Every time you answer a question in class, a group of other students starts laughing at you and whispering to each other.

2. Discuss with students the strategy that finally worked to stop Grant from bullying everyone – sticking together and standing up to him. Explain to students that they are always more likely to be bullied if and when they are alone, because they are easy targets. Yet if they stick together and form a group, bullies will almost always feel threatened by this and will leave them alone. Bullies get power from picking on people who they don't think can – or will – stand up for themselves. Tell students you'd like to show them a visual example of how effective this strategy is. Ask for a student volunteer to come to the front of the class and hand the student a pencil. Tell the student you'd like them to break the pencil in half – they will look at you as if you're crazy, but encourage them to do it. The pencil should break easily. Now hand the same student a handful of pencils (8-12) and ask the student to break them. The student will most likely say that he'll be able to break the pencils with no trouble, and he will likely get plenty of peer pressure from friends to do so, but he won't be able to do it. Reiterate to students that there is always strength in numbers.

Activity with Reproducible

As a class, ask students to brainstorm different ways to stop a bully. Write their ideas on the board and ask each student who contributes an idea to act out that idea (or someone else can act it out if the student isn't comfortable doing so). For example – If a student suggests "tell the bully to stop," ask that student to show you exactly how they would tell the bully – in what tone of voice, using what specific body language, etc. When the students run out of ideas, add some of your own to the list if you have any they haven't already mentioned. Give each student a Block the Bully Bingo sheet and ask them to look at their words from the board as well as the list on the sheet and write a strategy in each blank square. Make sure students understand that they have to write the strategies they choose in random fashion on their bingo cards, in order for the game to work. Once all students have filled up their cards, have them tear off small pieces of notebook paper to use as covers, and begin calling the game. Allow enough time for several students to "win" at Bully Bingo. When someone wins, ask them to stand up, read their answers aloud and share which two strategies (of the four) they would feel most comfortable using.

Block the Bully Bingo

Directions: *Using the list of bully blocking strategies your class came up with and the strategies listed below, write one strategy in each blank square. Make sure you write your strategies in random order on your bingo card so you don't end up with the same exact card as someone else.*

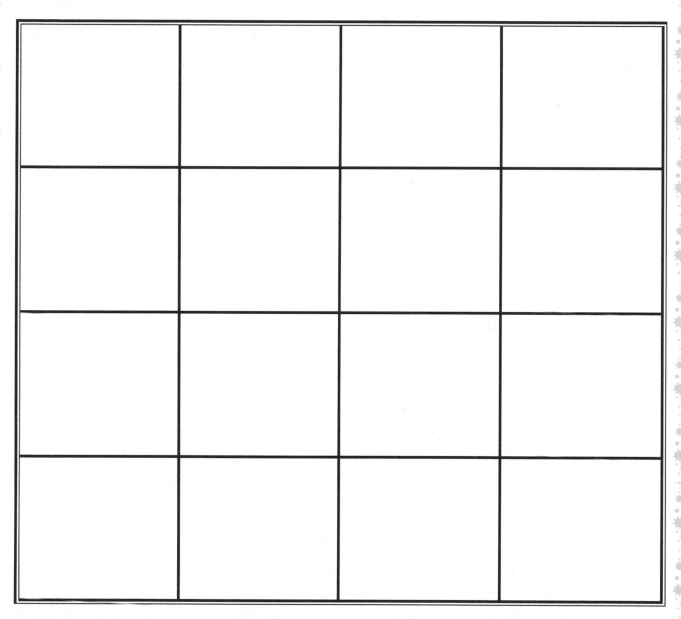

Ask for help

Shrug it off

Talk to your parents

Speak out loudly

Tell the bully to stop

Use an I-message

Ignore the bully

Talk to a counselor

Look bully in the eye

Join up with other kids

Include everyone

Be nice to the bully

Use your words

Stand up to the bully

Help others being bullied

Walk away

Celebrating Differences

Classrooms around the country are becoming increasingly diverse. Inclusion models are integrating students with physical and educational differences into mainstream classrooms. Children are often fearful of what they don't understand, and it's difficult for students to understand differences if they haven't been exposed to others who are different. Students' life experiences, cultural norms, skin color, family traditions, language, food, music and clothing all contribute to their understanding of and appreciation for each other. Students need to be taught that being different is not bad, and that our differences are what make us unique.

These books invite students to carefully examine their own unique qualities, as well as the qualities of those around them. They promote themes of respect, celebration, awareness and sensitivity. Instilling these values at a young age will prove beneficial for both the child and our communities.

Odd Velvet

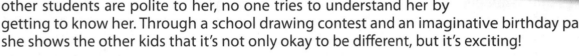

Book: *Odd Velvet* by Mary E. Whitcomb

Publisher: Chronicle Books

Grade Levels: 2-5

Setting: Individual, Group, Classroom

Book Description

Velvet is not like the other kids in the class. She does not wear a new dress on the first day of school, she eats (and enjoys) healthy food, and she brings in milkweed pods for show and tell. Although the other students are polite to her, no one tries to understand her by getting to know her. Through a school drawing contest and an imaginative birthday party, she shows the other kids that it's not only okay to be different, but it's exciting!

Materials Needed

- ***Activity with Reproducible** - copies of the reproducible activity, crayons*

Preparation

- ***Extension Activity #1** - divide students into pairs*
- ***Extension Activity #2** - reserve a large, open space for the class*

Introduction

Write the word *odd* on the board and ask students if they have ever heard of this word and/or know what it means. Gather student responses. If students need prompting, offer synonyms like "different, strange or unusual." Next, ask them if odd sounds like a positive or negative word. Explain that you are going to read a story about a girl who was odd. Tell them that at the end of the story, you will ask them to decide if being odd was positive or negative in this story.

Follow-up Questions (after reading)

1. In what ways was Velvet different from the other students?

2. Do you think Velvet realized that she was different than the other students? Do you think this bothered her?

3. How did the drawing contest change the way the students viewed Velvet?

4. If you had to describe Velvet using three adjectives, what adjectives would you use? (brave, imaginative, confident, etc.)

5. Do you think kids are afraid to be different from their classmates? Explain.

Extension Activities

1. Divide the students into groups of two. Pair students up with someone they typically do not spend much time with. Explain that they will be interviewing their designated classmate to find out three things that they don't already know about that person. As a group, brainstorm ten possible questions that they could ask their partner. Write them on the board so that students can access them during their interview. When they have finished their interviews, invite everyone back to the reading area. Allow students to share the three fun facts that they learned about their partner.

2. Here is an active game that is sure to be a crowd pleaser! If the classroom does not have a large, open space, try to arrange space in the PE room, cafeteria or on the playground. Ask students to sit in a large circle. Explain to the students that they are going to play a game titled "Mix it up!" In this game, one student stands in the middle of the circle, leaving their seat vacant in the circle. That student should think of one personal quality or talent that he is proud of and is willing to share with the group. After the student shares it with the group, he should say loudly, "Mix it up!" If there is anyone else in the group that shares that same quality or talent, they should stand up, go to the middle of the circle and try to steal the seat of someone else who also stood up. The person who doesn't have a seat is the next person to stand in the middle of the circle and share their special quality or talent. This is a great way to reinforce the idea that our differences make us stronger!

Activity with Reproducible

Ask students to think about two things that make them unique. Maybe they have an unusual talent, traveled to a far away country or enjoy an unpopular food (like liver)! Tell them to try to think of two things that nobody else knows about them. Ask them to keep these two facts a secret because they will be playing a game to see if they can guess which facts belong to which person. Hand out the activity sheet and go over the directions. Ask students to spread out in the classroom to complete the activity. When they are finished, tell them to hand in their paper to a neutral location. When all of the students are finished, ask them to gather back at the reading area. Read the students' papers and ask them to guess who wrote each one. Have fun learning about the unique personalities in the classroom. Consider hanging the papers on a bulletin board with the heading "Celebrating our Differences!"

"Did You Know..."

Directions: *Think about two little known facts that no one else knows about you. Maybe you like an unpopular food. Maybe you traveled to an exotic country? Write each fact on the lines below and include illustrations. Remember to keep these fun facts a secret until you gather together as a class.*

I _____

_____

_____.

I also_____

_____

_____.

Name _____

Stellaluna

Book: *Stellaluna* by Janell Cannon

Publisher: Houghton Mifflin Harcourt

Grade Levels: 1-3

Setting: Large Group, Classroom

Book Description

When Stellaluna, a baby fruit bat, gets separated from her mother, she falls headfirst into a baby bird's nest. She quickly befriends the three baby birds, but her world is literally turned upside down as she tries to adapt to the habits and rituals of her new friends. This is a heartwarming story about similarities, differences and the importance of self-acceptance.

Materials Needed

- *Extension Activity #1 -* one red apple for every student (if apples are out of season, you can substitute plums)
- *Extension Activity #2 -* old crayons in approximately 15 different colors (divide the number of students in the class by two in order to decide how many crayons you'll need)
- *Extension Activity #3 -* a large box of crayons

Preparation

- *Extension Activity #2 -* Break the old crayons in half ahead of time.
- *Activity with Reproducible -* Let the classroom teacher know ahead of time that you'll be doing a lesson on accepting differences. Ask the teacher to prepare a list of student pairs who normally don't interact with each other.

Introduction

Have children join you in the reading area. Tell students you're going to ask them a series of questions that they will respond to by raising their hands and that you'd like them to carefully watch each other as they do so. Have students raise their hands if they: are in 2nd grade (or whatever grade you're working with), have an older brother or sister, have a younger brother or sister, like pizza, like math, have green eyes, like cartoons, have a pet, live in a white house, have ever been on a plane, etc. After you're asked all your questions, ask students what they noticed about each other. Lead them to a discussion about individual differences and similarities – what were some things they all had in common? What were some ways they differed from each other? Invite two volunteers to come to the front of the room, and ask students to find some similarities and differences between the two students. Ask children how it helps to be different from each other, and how it helps to have things in common. Encourage them to think about what the world would be like if everyone dressed, talked and acted exactly like they did, and if everyone had exactly the same interests. Tell students you will be reading them a story about some animals that were different from each other but were still able to be friends.

Follow-up Questions (after reading)

1. How was Stellaluna the same as her bird friends? How was she different? Which was better?

2. How were Stellaluna's differences helpful to the birds?

3. What did the birds teach Stellaluna? What did she teach them?

4. How did Stellaluna try to fit in? Why did she try to fit in?

5. How could their differences have caused problems? Did they learn to appreciate each other's differences in the end? How do you know?

6. Can you be friends with someone very different from you? (Help children understand that our differences are what help us learn from each other)

Extension Activities

1. Give each student an apple. Tell them you're going to give them two minutes to study their apple very closely and "get to know it." After the two minutes is up, collect all the apples in a small basket. Ask students to raise their hand if they feel they really got to know their apple, and ask them if they think they could pick their apple out of the crowd. Pass the basket back around and allow two or three students at a time to choose "their" apple from the bunch. Once all students are satisfied that they've reunited with their apple, give students a chance to comment on how the differences among apples helped to identify them. Discuss with students that while the apples all look a little bit different, they are also very much the same. The differences don't make them better or worse than one another, and their similarities help them be connected to each other and recognized as a group. Have students share what would have happened if all the apples were exactly identical. When students have finished their discussion, allow them to wash their apples and eat them.

2. Give each student half of a crayon. Let students walk around the room until they find their match – whoever has the other half of their crayon. As each student finds her partner, have each pair sit down together. Explain to students that one thing that can help us respect and understand each other is to get to know each other better. Give students five minutes to talk with their partner about things they have in common and things that make them different. To help students get started, you might want to write a list of possible conversation starters on the board: favorite food, favorite TV show, number of siblings, favorite hobby, favorite season, favorite subject, etc. Then go around the room and let each pair have a turn to tell one thing they have in common with each other and one difference they have.

3. Show students a large box of crayons. Ask students why they think there are so many different colors in a box. Ask how many of them have used crayons to draw a picture or to color in a coloring book. Ask how many of them use many different colors to complete their picture, instead of just one color. Give several students an opportunity to share why they use multiple colors in their drawings. Point out to students that if we always just used one color in our pictures and drawings, our pictures would be boring and dull – the more colors we add, the brighter and more dynamic the picture is.

Activity with Reproducible

Reiterate to students that no matter who they meet in life, they are always likely to find more in common with people than they are likely to find differences. However, when there are differences, these should be celebrated, because our differences are what make us unique.

Put students in pairs to complete their activity sheet, and give one activity sheet to each pair. Explain to them that they are going to get to know their partner better, and that you want them to each find three things they have in common with their partner and three differences they have. You will probably need to give students some "hints" for conversation topics (family, favorite foods, TV shows, favorite class, hobbies, colors, places visited, etc.) Remind students how important it is to listen closely to each other so they don't miss any important information. Tell students you'd like them to write the things they have in common with their partner in the middle of the bat, and the things that make each of them different on each side of the bat (the wings).

We Are Different Yet The Same

Things That Make Me Different

THINGS THAT MAKE US THE SAME

Things That Make Me Different

REPRODUCIBLE WORKSHEET

The Skin You Live In

Book: *The Skin You Live In* by Michael Tyler

Publisher: Chicago Children's Museum

Target Grades: K-2

Setting: Small Group, Classroom

Book Description

This colorful book, written in poetic form, celebrates the many different shades of skin that we all live in. In the introduction, the author stresses the importance of diversity and encourages children to take pride in their own uniqueness. On the remaining pages, the author helps children understand that our identity is not limited to our skin color, and that our hopes, dreams, fears and imagination shape us into the wonderful creations that we are today. The figurative language and whimsical pictures make this a captivating book for children.

Materials Needed

- **Extension Activity #1 -** *hand-held mirror*
- **Extension Activity #2 -** *globe or map, sticky notes*
- **Activity with Reproducible -** *multi-cultural crayons, reproducible copied on cardstock paper, glue or stapler, bulletin board paper*

Preparation

- **Extension Activity #2 -** *Contact parents, if needed* .

Introduction

Invite children to sit in a circle so they can easily view all of their classmates. Ask them to look very carefully at each one of their classmates, noticing their hair, clothing and skin. Ask students to brainstorm and identify at least five ways the group is similar and five ways they are different. Compile their list on the board. If the students do not mention skin color as one of their differences, prompt them by asking if their skin colors are all the same. Show the book and explain that they are going to hear a wonderful story that celebrates all the different colors of skin that are represented in their group.

Follow-up Questions (after reading)

1. What did you notice about the children in the book? Did they look the same or were they different?

2. Would the book be interesting if all of the children looked the same? Explain.

3. Why do you think we all have different skin colors?

4. Did you see the girl that was sitting in the special chair? Do you know the name of that special chair? Do you know anyone who uses a wheelchair or have you seen a wheelchair when you were at a restaurant, store, etc.? How do wheelchairs help people?

Extension Activities

1. Pass the hand-held mirror around the circle. Ask each student to look carefully at the color of their beautiful skin. In the book, the author related skin colors to different types of food, such as "coffee and cream skin" or "marshmallow treat skin." Ask each student to name a food that reminds them of the color of their skin. If they have trouble, allow them to use the food examples from the book. *Optional* – Bring in some of the food mentioned in the book to spark the students' imagination!

2. Show students a world map or globe. Explain that all of our families came to America from different parts of the world. Introduce the word *ancestors* and explain that our ancestors all came to America for different reasons. Often, our skin color reflects our ancestors' birthplace. For homework, ask students to go home and ask their families where their ancestors lived before they came to America. *A word of caution:* Be sensitive to adoptive children in your class. You may want to consider contacting these parents before you read the book so that they can be prepared for their children's questions. When students return the next day, ask them to report back about their country or countries of origin. Place a sticky note or small sticker on the map to represent that country (or countries). When everyone has reported, step back to look at all of the countries that are represented in your class.

Activity with Reproducible

After reading the book, ask children to go back to their tables. Hand out boxes of multicultural crayons to each table. Ask children how these boxes of crayons are different than their usual boxes of crayons. Explain that these crayons represent different colors of skin.

Ask children if they have ever seen a quilt on a bed or hanging in their house. Tell students that patchwork quilts are beautiful because they are made of different-colored patches that are sewn together. Explain that the class is going to make a "Celebrating our Skin" Patchwork Quilt.

Distribute a patch to each student. Ask students to draw a picture of their face, using the crayon that shows their skin color. Allow students to use the mirror if they want to look more closely at themselves.

When students are finished with their drawing, staple their patches together to make a classroom quilt. You can also glue the patches to a large sheet of bulletin board paper to create a year-long bulletin board display. Title the quilt, "Celebrating our Many Colors!"

Celebrating Our Many Colors

Name _____

© YouthLight, Inc.

The Sneetches

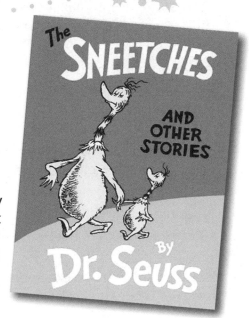

Book: *The Sneetches* by Dr. Seuss

Publisher: Random House

Target Grades: 3-5

Setting: Classroom

Book Description

The Star-Belly Sneetches think they are far superior to the Plain-Belly Sneetches. They brag about their appearance and refuse to interact with any Sneetch who doesn't have a star on his belly. When Sylvester McMonkey McBean comes to town and tricks all the Sneetches out of their money, they learn just how foolish they were to judge each other on their appearance. This book addresses cliques and exclusion in a way children can easily relate to.

Materials Needed

- ***Extension Activity #1** - green dots or green foil stars (*Do this activity before reading the book.)*
- ***Extension Activity #2** - multi-colored "garage sale" dots – You will need three or four different colors. You need enough dots so there are at least three children in the classroom with each color dot. You will also need one color that only one student will get.*

Preparation

- ***Activity with Reproducible -** Copy the star on green paper (one star per student).*

Introduction

Ask students how important they think looks are when making new friends. Most children will say looks aren't important at all, and that they don't decide whether or not to be friends with someone based on that person's beauty or clothing – although many of these same students feel they **have** to have a particular brand or style of clothing or shoes in order to fit in.

Ask students how many of them have heard of cliques, and ask several different students to give you their definition of a clique. Discuss the following questions with students: How and why are cliques started? How do cliques treat those on "the outside" and why? How can cliques be hurtful to others? What can you do to stop cliques from forming? How many of you have ever felt included by a clique? Excluded by a clique? Give children an opportunity to talk about how they felt when they were left out. Tell students you will be sharing a book with them about a group whose feelings are hurt because they are excluded because of their appearance. Before reading, tell students you'd like them to think about the fact that when we try so hard to be like other people, instead of being happy with who we are, it never ends well.

Follow-up Questions (after reading)

1. How did the Star-Belly Sneetches treat the Plain-Belly Sneetches? Why did they treat them this way? Was this fair? How do you think this made the Plain-Belly-Sneetches feel?

2. How do you think the Plain-Belly Sneetches felt when Sylvester McMonkey McBean offered to give them stars – for a small fee? Why do you think they felt this way? How did they feel after they showed their stars to the Star-Belly Sneetches?

3. Why do you think it was so important to the Star-Belly Sneetches to have their stars removed by Mr. McBean's contraption? Can you think of a real-life example of people who are like the Star-Belly Sneetches?

4. Do you think Mr. McBean was honest or dishonest? Do you think he really cared about the Sneetches? What do you think his main reason was for "helping" the Sneetches?

5. What did it take for the Sneetches to finally realize it didn't matter whether or not they had stars? Do you think they learned anything from their experience?

6. How can students be like Sneetches? Can you think of some things you could do to help other people feel special and included?

Extension Activities

1. * This activity works best if done before reading the book. As students come to the reading area, walk around and place a green star sticker – or green dot – on half of the students' foreheads or hands, but don't tell them why. Engage students in "small talk" for a couple of minutes to distract them from the green dots. Then make a list of privileges on the board – examples might include going to get a drink of water, getting a piece of candy, being called on first, sitting at the front of the reading area, getting invited to lunch with the counselor, etc. For the students that have green stars, call on them individually and award them with one – or more – of the privileges, without acknowledging any of the students without stars. It might take awhile for students to catch on to what you're doing – but don't let on that anything is out of the ordinary. OR….give half the group star stickers ahead of time and make them feel important during a group discussion by asking specific questions (about favorite hobbies, foods, etc.) and only calling on those who have stars. Then change it so only those without stars are important and get to answer similar questions. Afterward, ask students to share how they felt when they were included, and how they felt when they were excluded.

2. Tell students you will be walking around and placing a colored dot sticker on each of their foreheads, but that they can't look at the color of it, and they're not allowed to ask anyone else what color it is. Go around the room silently, and place a dot on each student's forehead. **Make sure that the student who gets the one different colored dot is an outgoing and well-liked student (this is crucial). After all the dots have been placed on students' foreheads, tell students you'd like them to walk around the room until they've figured out – by asking others – what group they belong to. After several minutes, the groups will be formed, and there will be one student who doesn't fit in any of the groups. Lead a discussion with students about how it feels to be different from everyone else, how it feels to be left out of a group, and how it feels to be included in one. Ask the rest of the group to express their feelings on what they saw happening. Discuss ways that students can make sure others in their school are always included.

Activity with Reproducible

Ask students to either sit in a circle on the floor, or have them sit at their desks and push the desks into a circle. Give all students one green star and ask them to write their name at the top of the star. On the back of their star, have them write one thing they like about themselves that **isn't** related to appearance. Ask students to flip their stars back to the side with their name, and then pass their star to the person on their right. Tell students you would like them to look at the name on the star they're holding and write one thing they like about that person – and again, it can't be related to appearance (or possessions) in any way. Once they've written on that star, have them pass the star along again to the person on their right. Encourage students to think about positive experiences they've had themselves with that particular student, rather than just copying what other people have written. After all the stars have been around the circle, collect them to verify that all comments written were positive and appropriate, and return them to their owners. Have students volunteer to share their stars with the class – or you can volunteer to read aloud the stars yourself, if students are more comfortable with that. After all the stars are shared, ask students to call out how they feel about themselves after reading their stars. Emphasize the importance of looking for the good inside others, rather than making judgments based on outward appearances.

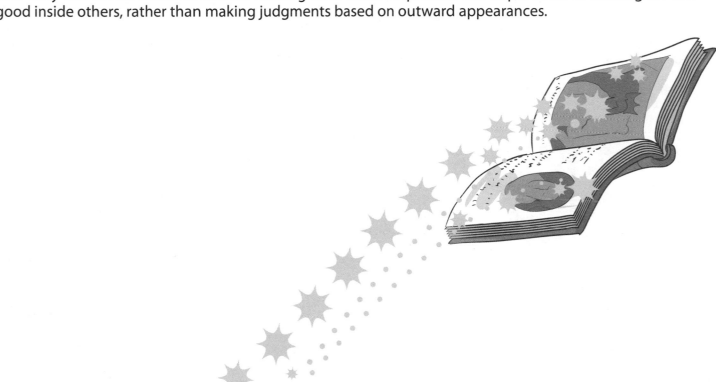

I'm a Star!

Directions: *Write your name at the top of the star. On the back of your star write one thing you like about yourself that isn't related to appearance. Then flip your star over to the side with your name and pass it to the person on your right. The person to your right should write one thing they like about you - not related to appearance (or possessions) in any way. Once they have written on your star, have them pass your star along again to the person on their right. By the time everyone has passed their stars around, everyone will have written something positive about everyone else – including you! When writing comments, please try to think about positive experiences you have had with each particular student, rather than just copying what others have written.*

Cooperation and Sharing

Every early childhood teacher knows the importance of cooperation and sharing. They know it is imperative for students to learn these skills at a young age as it creates a classroom environment where children can work and play in harmony. Parents also understand the importance of cooperation and sharing because having a cooperative and sharing child makes everything from play dates and family vacations to household chores more peaceful and productive.

For these reasons, all of the books and lesson plans in this section are geared toward early childhood students. However, they can be easily adapted for upper elementary-aged children because, as we know, themes of cooperation and sharing sometimes need to be revisited as children reach new developmental stages. The hands-on activities presented here reinforce cooperation and sharing through play, art and role plays.

It's Mine

Book: *It's Mine* by Leo Lionni

Publisher: Dragonfly Books

Grade Levels: K-2

Setting: Individual, Group, Classroom

Book Description

Milton, Rupert and Lydia are three bickering frogs who argue with each other all day long. They argue about who owns the water, who owns the air and who gets to eat the worm. One day, a wise toad visits the pond and teaches them an important lesson about sharing and the comfort that comes from sticking together.

Materials Needed

- **Extension Activity #1 -** *large hula hoops, radio or CD player*
- **Activity with Reproducible -** *crayons/markers, pencils*

Preparation: None needed

Introduction

Ask students to come to the reading area. Show the book cover and tell them that they are going to hear a story about three selfish frogs. Ask if any students have ever heard of the word *selfish*. Do they know what it means? Explain that if you do not share with other people, your friends may tell you that you are being selfish. Tell students that in this book, they will see how three frogs learn an important lesson about sharing and sticking together.

Follow-up Questions (after reading)

1. What do Rupert, Milton and Lydia argue about in the book?

2. How did the toad teach them an important lesson about sharing?

3. Is it easy or hard to share? Which things are easy to share? Which things are hard to share?

4. Who do you have to share with in your life?

5. At the end of the book, the frogs' lives were peaceful. What made their lives peaceful?

Extension Activities

1. Using large hula hoops, play the "sharing version" of musical chairs. Arrange the hula hoops around the room and start the music. While the music is playing, ask the students to hop around the room like frogs. When the music stops, yell out a number. Tell students that each hula hoop must have at least that number of students in each of them. For example, if the number "2" is called, students must make sure that each hula hoop has at least two people in it. It may have more than two as long as all of the other hula hoops have two people. Explain that they will have to work together to solve the puzzle and share the hula hoops. Play the game several times, calling out different numbers each time.

2. Hold a "Share and Tell" day in the classroom. Ask students to think of one talent they have that they can share with the class. Tell students that it does not have to be something large, but rather something that they would enjoy "teaching" to the rest of the class. For example, maybe they know how to draw a really good dinosaur. Maybe they have a favorite song they would like to teach the class. The only requirement is that it has to be a talent they currently have that they can teach the class in 2-3 minutes. Allow students a "three minute spotlight" as they share their talent with the class. Remind students that sharing our talents is a win-win situation for everyone.

Activity with Reproducible

Ask students to think about one of their possessions that is very hard for them to share with a friend or sibling. Distribute the activity sheet and ask students to draw a picture of themselves sharing that particular possession with their friend and/or sibling. Ask them to finish the sentence prompts or have them dictate the sentence as you write it for them. Have students share their finished artwork and challenge them to work extra hard on sharing with their friends. They will hopefully experience the same happiness as Milton, Rupert and Lydia at the end of the story!

"It's Mine... but I'll Share it With You!"

Directions: *Think about one of your possessions that is hard for you to share with someone else. Maybe it's your favorite toy or book? Or it's a favorite space, such as your bedroom or playroom? Draw a picture of you sharing this item or space and fill in the sentence below.*

In this picture, I am sharing _____

_____

with _____

_____.

Name _____

Swimmy

Book: *Swimmy* by Leo Lionni

Publisher: Scholastic Inc.

Grade Levels: K-2

Setting: Individual, Group, Classroom

Book Description

Swimmy the Fish finds himself orphaned after a big tuna feasts on his brothers and sisters. Scared and alone, Swimmy scrapes up the courage to venture out and discover all the wonderful treasures of the sea. When he meets up with a school of fish, he encourages them to come with him on his adventure. When they voice concern about being eaten by the larger sea creatures, Swimmy teaches them to conquer their fears through cooperation and creative problem-solving.

Materials Needed

- ***Extension Activity #1 -*** *Goldfish® Crackers*
- ***Extension Activity #2 -*** *chart paper*
- ***Extension Activity #3 -*** *Legos™ or blocks*
- ***Activity with Reproducible -*** *small boxes of crayons, activity sheet copied on 11x17 paper*

Preparation

- ***Extension Activity #1 -*** *Before the students enter the classroom, hide goldfish at various spots in the classroom.*
- ***Activity with Reproducible -*** *Copy the activity sheet on 11x17 paper.*

Introduction

Invite students to come to the reading area and ask them to raise their hand if they like to play games with their friends. Gather their responses. Explain that playing games and working together in the classroom requires cooperation. Ask them if they have ever heard of the word *cooperation* or know what it means. Tell students that you are going to read a book about a very smart fish who taught his friends the importance of cooperation.

Follow-up Questions (after reading)

1. How do you think Swimmy felt after his brothers and sisters were eaten by the tuna?

2. When he met up with the new school of fish, he asked them to come on the adventure with him. Why didn't they want to go with him?

3. Have you ever been scared to try something new? Explain.

4. Would you call Swimmy a good problem solver? What problem(s) did he solve?

5. How did the fish cooperate with one another? What do you think would have happened if they had not cooperated with one another?

Extension Activities

1. Before the students arrive, hide a certain number of Goldfish® Crackers at various spots in the classroom. It works well to hide one Goldfish® Cracker per child. After reading the story, tell students that you have a special challenge for them. You will give them five minutes to find all of the goldfish that you hid around the room (tell them the amount of fish that they are looking for). Designate a specific location for them to put the fish when they have been "found." Ask one person to be the counter and keep track of their findings. At the end of the five minutes, gather the students together to count their total. If they reached their goal, ask them if they think they would have been able to find all of the fish without the help of their classmates. Explain to them that sometimes we are more powerful as a group than by ourselves. If they did not reach their goal, ask them if they thought they were doing a good job of cooperating with one another. Gather responses. Give them another 2-3 minutes to see if they can locate the remaining goldfish. Due to germs, throw away these fish and treat students to a handful of (fresh) Goldfish® Crackers at their seat!

2. On a large piece of chart paper, ask students to create a list of "cooperating words." These are words that people use when they are cooperating with each other. Encourage students to come up with at least ten. Examples include "Let's work together" and "Good job. Don't give up!"

3. Divide students into small groups of 4-6 students. Using Legos or blocks, challenge students to work together to create a real or imaginary animal. They must work together to create one animal (instead of 4-6 smaller animals). Ask them to name the animal and share it with the class.

Activity with Reproducible

Divide students into small groups of 4-6 students. Distribute one box of crayons and a copy of the fish reproducible to each group. You may want to enlarge the reproducible onto 11x17 paper. Explain that they have 15 minutes to color the fish as a group. They will have to decide which colors to use on the picture, delegate who colors each section, and share the one box of crayons (the smaller the box of crayons, the better). Tell students that you will be circulating around the room to see which groups are cooperating with each other. Designate one student in the group to be the "problem solver." This student helps mediate any problems that arise during the activity. Allow groups to share their picture when everyone is finished.

Cooperation Coloring Challenge

The Little Red Hen

Book: *The Little Red Hen and the Ear of Wheat* by Mary Finch

Publisher: Barefoot Books

Grade Levels: K-2

Setting: Small group or classroom

Book Description

A rooster and a mouse live with the little red hen and lazily refuse to help plant, water, harvest and grind a grain of wheat to turn it into a loaf of bread. When the little red hen won't share the loaf of bread with her uncooperative friends, they learn their lesson, and decide to cooperate the next time, so they too, can have some bread.

Materials Needed

- *Extension Activity #1 - 8 oz. carton of heaving whipping cream, a "pinch" of salt, a clear, plastic container with a tightly sealed top, and a small box of crackers*
- *Extension Activity #2 - crayons and drawing paper*
- *Extension Activity #3 - hula hoop*
- *Activity with Reproducible - glue sticks, white paper*

Preparation

- *Activity with Reproducible - Copy and cut out the sequencing blocks ahead of time and make sure each group is given the correct four sequencing blocks.*

Introduction

Ask students if they've ever heard of the word cooperation, and if anyone can tell you what it might mean. If nobody guesses correctly, explain that cooperation means working together to get a job or task done. Tell students that you're going to read them a story about three animal friends and you'd like them to listen for whether or not the animals are cooperating with each other.

Follow-up Questions (after reading)

1. Who did the Little Red Hen ask for help? Who do *you* ask for help?

2. What did she want help with? What things do *you* sometimes need help with?

3. Why didn't the rooster and mouse want to help? Has there ever been a time when you didn't want to help someone? How do you think the Little Red Hen felt when they wouldn't help?

4. What **did** the rooster and mouse want to help with? Why?

5. If you were the Little Red Hen, would you have shared the bread?

6. What happened when everyone cooperated? Why is it important to cooperate with others?

7. Tell about some ways you can cooperate at home? At school?

Extension Activities

1. Have students sit in a circle. Pour about ¼ - ½ of the cream into the container and add a pinch of salt. Tell them that they are going to cooperate in order to make a type of food that they will then get to eat. Ask if any of them can guess what they might be making. Most students think the cream is milk, and several of them will likely guess that they'll be making a milkshake or ice cream. When you explain that the "milk," is cream, and that they'll be turning it into butter by working together to shake it as hard as they can, they get very excited. After you shake the container vigorously for several turns, teach children the following cheer, and have the group recite the cheer as the container is passed from child to child. *"Go cream go, shake, shake, shake, We all work together, and butter we will make."*

   Depending on the size of the group, and also on how hard the children shake the container, you will probably have to go around the circle three to five times before the cream turns into a true butter consistency (to speed up the process a little, it sometimes helps to add a couple of small ice cubes). You'll probably also have to do a lot of vigorous shaking yourself. When the butter is ready, open the container and show the students what they've made together by cooperating. Then spread some butter on the crackers so every child can have a chance to taste what they made.

2. Pair students up and give each pair one box of crayons and one piece of paper. Tell students that you want them to work with their partner to draw a picture that fills up the whole paper. Explain to them that they may draw anything they choose, but that somewhere in their picture they have to include a circle, a square and a triangle. Once the pictures have been completed, have students come together in a circle and ask them the following questions: 1) Was sharing one piece of paper easy or hard, 2) Did one of you do most of the drawing or talking? 3) Did anyone disagree with their partner about part or all of the drawing?

3. Have all students stand in a circle and hold hands with each other. Place a large hula hoop between two people (sitting on their clasped hands). Explain to students that the goal of the activity is to have the hula hoop travel around the entire circle without anyone unclasping their hands. Most students at first will exclaim that this isn't possible – you can either show them how it works, or encourage them to figure it out themselves. Most students will figure out pretty quickly that they have to shimmy and wiggle the hula hoop to get it up their arm, over their shoulder, neck and head, and down their other arm. Once the hula hoop has made it all the way around the circle, ask students "who won?" This should naturally lead into a discussion that the entire group is working together, and that there are no winners or losers.

Activity with Reproducible

Review the definition of cooperation with students. Remind students how tasks are much easier and quicker when we can work together on them. Help students understand that when we work together, we all bring different strengths to the group. Divide students into groups of four and give each group the four cut up squares from the activity sheet, a glue stick, and a piece of paper. Tell students they must work together to put the pictures in the right order, based on what they remember from the book. When all students are finished, give them time to share their page, and ask each group to give you a thumbs up, thumbs sideways or thumbs down to show how well their group worked together.

What Happens Next?

Directions: Work as a team to put the following four squares in the correct order based on the book. Once they are in the right order, use your glue stick to glue them to the paper.

© YouthLight, Inc.

The Rainbow Fish

Book: *The Rainbow Fish* by Marcus Pfister

Publisher: Scholastic Inc.

Grade Levels: K-2

Setting: Large Group or Classroom

Book Description

Rainbow Fish's beautiful shiny scales set him apart from the other fish. When he refuses to give one of his special scales to another fish, the wise octopus teaches him an important lesson about sharing. As soon as Rainbow Fish gives one away, he gets "hooked" on sharing the beauty of his scales with all the fish in the sea.

Materials Needed

- *Extension Activity #1 - gummy fish candy and aluminum foil*
- *Extension Activity #2 - fruit cereal loops, 1 piece of thin string for each child, roll of tape*

Preparation

- *Extension Activity #1 - Before the class starts, wrap Gummy fish in aluminum foil. Wrap some fish individually – and include two or three fish in other packages. Make sure you have fewer fish than the number of students.*
- *Extension Activity #2 - Write each student's name on a small piece of paper, fold it in half, and place it in a small container. Make a friendship necklace ahead of time to show students as an example.*

Introduction

Invite students to the reading area and show them the cover of the book. Ask if they notice anything unique (the silvery scales of the fish) and if they have any ideas what the book is about. Tell students you're going to be talking about a very important topic today, but you'd like them to guess what the topic is after they hear the story.

Follow-up Questions (after reading)

1. How did Rainbow Fish feel about his scales in the beginning of the story? Ask several students to share something they own that they are attached to.

2. Why wouldn't Rainbow Fish give any of his scales away? Can you think of a time it was hard for you to share with someone else?

3. How did the little blue fish feel when Rainbow Fish wouldn't give him a scale? How do you feel when someone doesn't share with you?

4. Why did Rainbow Fish visit the wise Octopus? What advice did the Octopus give? Do you think it was good advice?

5. How did Rainbow Fish feel when he started sharing? How did it make the other fish feel? How does it make you feel when you share with other people?

6. Is it easy or hard to share? Do you think sharing with others is a good way to make friends?

Extension Activities

1. Tell students that they're going to go on a treasure hunt. Explain that you've hidden some special silver packages around the room, and you'd like for students to find them. Tell them they must hold the packages very carefully (to go along with the feel of a real treasure hunt). Ask them to return to the group circle if they find a silver package. Once all the students are seated again, there will be several disappointed or upset faces from students who didn't find a "treasure." Initially, pretend that you don't notice the fact that students are upset, and brightly ask if everyone is excited about finding a treasure. Of course, the students who found the packages will be excited, and those who didn't will tell you that they didn't find anything. Explain to them that maybe they'll have a turn at finding the treasure another day. Then have the students who found the packages slowly open them in front of everyone. Point out (as if to yourself) that some of the packages have only one fish, but some have two or three. Ask the students if it's fair that some students have two or three fish and some have none. They all agree that it doesn't seem fair, and after a few minutes, they usually come up with the idea (on their own) to share the fish with each other. Allow them to eat the fish once everyone has at least one.

2. Explain to children that they will be making friendship necklaces to share with someone in their class. Show an example of a necklace you have already made. Note: Students will not get to decide who to give their necklace to – after they make the necklace they will draw a name. This way all students are included and nobody has hurt feelings. Have a piece of string taped at the top of each student's desk. Give each group of students a pile of fruit loops to share while making the necklaces. After all students have finished, have them sit in a circle as a class, with their necklaces in front of them on the floor. Discuss how each necklace is different and special. Select one student (I always look for the best listener) to come up and draw a name from the container. This student should walk over to the child he picked and give her the friendship necklace. Tell students that when they give their necklace away, they must share one nice comment with the student who's receiving the necklace. (Thanks for being my friend, I like when you _____, etc.) The child who receives the necklace must also say thank you. The next child to draw a name is the one who just received a necklace. When everyone has received a necklace, ask students how it felt to give their necklaces away, and how it felt to receive a new necklace. Students may either choose to keep their necklaces, or eat them!

Activity with Reproducible

Ask students to give you some examples of friendship qualities that were demonstrated in the story, and write these examples on the board. Have students share some examples of friendship that they have shown others, or that others have shown them, and write these responses on the board as well. Encourage students to be specific when naming friendship characteristics – instead of "nice," they could say "friendly," or "smiling," for example. Students can give one word qualities, or they can use phrases, such as "invites me to play with them." Once you've collected a sufficient number of responses, give students a fish scale and ask them to draw an example of a way they can be a good friend – and have them write their word or phrase at the bottom. When all students have completed their fish scales, they can be put together into one large fish – or a school of fish – for display in the classroom or hall.

Friendship Fish Scale

Directions: Draw a picture inside the fish scale of one way you can be a good friend. Then write a word or sentence inside the fish scale that describes the friendship quality you drew. When you're done, cut out your fish scale and write your name at the bottom of the scale.

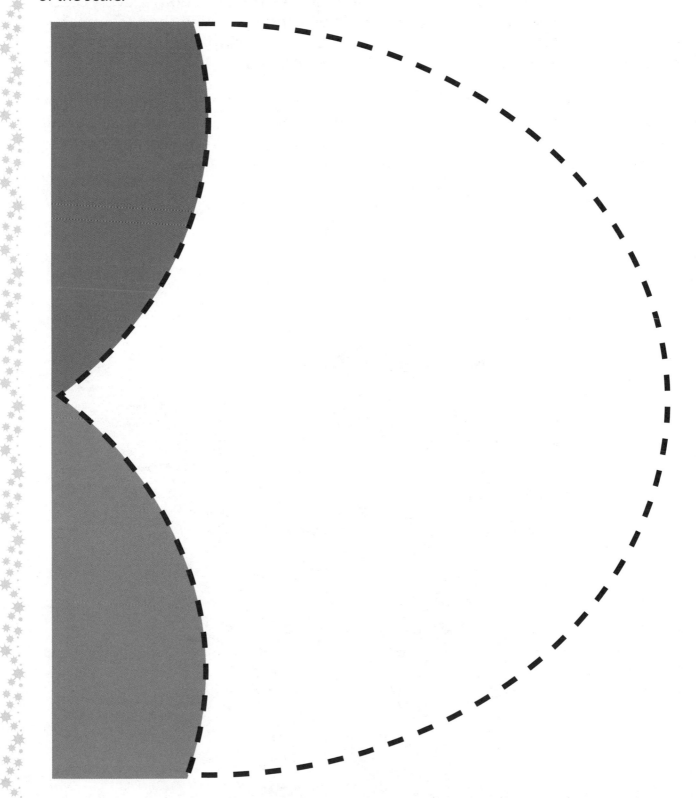

Feelings

All parents want their children to be able to persevere through difficult situations. Every teacher wants her students to be sensitive and kind to one another. Every coach desires players who are able to follow directions and work with their teammates, even when they do not see eye-to-eye. In order to develop these skills, children must be able to identify and manage all types of feelings.

There are a wide variety of books on this topic, so it was difficult to choose just four to highlight in this section. However, all of the books included emphasize that all feelings are okay, even those that are difficult to experience. They also demonstrate creative ways to manage and express feelings in a healthy manner.

Feelings to Share from A to Z

Book: *Feelings to Share from A to Z* by Todd and Peggy Snow

Grade Levels: Maren Green Publishing

Target Grades: K-2

Setting: Individual, Group, Classroom

Book Description

From **a**wesome to **z**any, this book provides a feeling word for every letter of the alphabet. Included with each feeling word is a short paragraph that explains when the reader might feel this way. The book includes both words that children easily recognize, such as *happy* and *mad*, and words they may not know such as *optimistic* and *generous*. Students will love the kid-friendly illustrations.

Materials Needed

- *Introduction* - large chart paper
- *Extension Activity #2* - 26 index cards, large chart paper
- *Activity with Reproducible* - bingo chips, bingo cards, copies of the second reproducible (if the students are too young to write the feeling words), scissors, glue sticks

Preparation

- *Activity with Reproducible* - Speak with the teacher to determine if the students are able to write the feeling words on the Bingo card. If this task is too difficult, make copies of the second reproducible.

Introduction

Ask students to come to the reading area. Explain that you will be reading a book titled *Feelings to Share from A to Z*. In the book, the authors provide a different feeling word for each letter of the alphabet. Ask students if they remember how many letters are in the alphabet. Can they believe that there are 26 different feeling words? Explain that you will write the feeling words in alphabetical order on the large chart paper so they can keep track of all of the words.

Follow-up Questions (after reading)

1. Did you learn any new feeling words from the story today? What was one of the words that you learned?

2. How can you tell how someone else is feeling? Are there any clues the person can give you without saying a word?

3. Did you notice that the illustrator used different colors with each feeling? Look at the color she used to illustrate mad (red). Do certain colors make you feel differently?

4. Do you think it is possible to feel more than one feeling at the same time? Can you tell us about a time when you experienced two of these feelings at the same time?

5. Where do your feelings live? Do they live in your tummy? Do they live in your fingers?

Extension Activities

1. Play Feelings Charades using the 26 feeling words from the story. Emphasizing to the students that we show our feelings with our bodies and our words, ask a student to volunteer and come to the front of the room. Explain that you will whisper one of the feeling words in the volunteer's ear. They will act out the word without speaking. The children have to be good detectives to figure out the feeling word. The first student to guess the word gets the opportunity to act out the next word.

2. Write 26 new feeling words on 3x5 index cards and hide them in various places around the room. Tell students that it is their job to look around the room to find the 26 feeling words, and that they're only allowed to pick up one feeling word (if you have more than 26 students in the class, some might have to double up.) After they have found all of the cards, call them back to the reading area. Using the same large chart paper from the lesson, ask each student to bring his feeling word forward when you call out the different letters of the alphabet. Read the feeling words together and discuss their meaning.

Activity with Reproducible

Play *Feelings Bingo* using the 26 feeling words from the book. Give each student a blank Bingo board and ask them to choose 16 of the feeling words to write on their individual board. Instruct them to stagger the words as they write them so that their board looks different than their neighbor's board. Hand out bingo chips or something similar, such as dried beans or poker chips. **Note:** If students are too young to write the words by themselves, photocopy the second reproducible. There are extra spaces for additional feeling words that you would like to add. Have the students cut apart the words and glue them on the Bingo cards. Call out the feeling words and play until one student gets four words in a row or until time runs out.

Sharing Our Feelings Bingo

Awesome	Brave	Creative	Dramatic	Exhausted
Frightened	Generous	Happy	Interested	Jealous
Kind	Lonely	Mad	Nervous	Optimistic
Proud	Quiet	Responsible	Shy	Thankful
Understood	Valued	Wishful	Excited	Yucky
Zany				

Glad Monster
Sad Monster

Book: *Glad Monster Sad Monster* by Ed Emberley and Anne Miranda

Publisher: L.B. Kids

Grade Levels: K-2

Setting: Individual, Small Group, Classroom

Book Description

This fun and engaging book addresses a variety of feelings children might have. A feeling mask accompanies every feeling illustrated in the book, so children can explore every different feeling in an interactive and non-threatening way.

Materials Needed

- ***Extension Activity #1 -*** *yellow and blue copy paper, wooden craft sticks, tape*
- ***Extension Activity #2 -*** *a large dice (any large block or cube with six sides will work)*

Preparation

- ***Extension Activity #1 -*** *Draw a large happy face and make copies of it on yellow paper, and draw a large sad/mad face and make copies of it on blue paper. Each child should have one happy face and one sad/mad face.*
- ***Extension Activity #2 -*** *Draw a feeling face for each of the following feelings – sad, happy, angry, scared, proud, and jealous – and tape a face to each side of the dice.*

Introduction

After greeting students, tell them you'd like them to share what kind of day they're having by showing you their thumbs. Explain to them that a "thumbs up" means they're having a great day, a "thumbs sideways" means their day is just so-so, and a "thumbs down" means they're having a bad day. Tally the results on the board, and discuss the outcome with students. Give students an opportunity to share why they're having a good/so-so/bad day, and ask them what might make their day better. Tell students you'd like to share a story with them about a group of monsters who have a lot of different feelings, and you'd like them to think about the feelings in the book that they feel most often.

*This book works best if, after reading it once to students, you go back through it a second time and ask for one volunteer at a time to come up and try on a feeling face mask. Let the student choose which mask he'd like to try on, and have him face the class in the mask, as the class tries to guess the feeling.

Follow-up Questions (after reading)

1. What were some of the feelings the monsters had?

2. What were some things that made the monsters happy? Sad? Angry? Scared? Silly?

3. Have you ever felt any of the same feelings the monsters did? What made you feel that way?

4. When you feel angry or sad, is there anyone or anything that can make you feel better? Who or what makes you feel better?

Extension Activities

1. Play the "How do you Feel" game. Give each student one happy face and one sad/mad face. (If time permits, you may let them cut out the faces and tape them to wooden craft sticks, pencils, etc.) As the following statements are read, ask children to hold up the face that matches how they would feel, and to call out the feeling they would have. Children might not always show the same feeling face – when this happens, point out that we all feel differently about things sometimes, and that the way we feel is never wrong.

   a) Your teacher says she's proud of how well you behaved in the assembly

   b) You accidentally fall down in P.E. and everyone laughs at you

   c) Your dad takes you to get ice cream after school

   d) Someone cuts in front of you in line

   e) You break your crayon and a classmate lets you borrow his crayon

   f) You overhear some other students talking about you

   g) Some kids in your class ask if you'd like to play with them at recess

   h) A student in your class is having a birthday party and everyone is invited except you

   i) You come to school with a new haircut and a student in your class says, "What happened to your hair?"

   j) The principal says hello to you when you get off the bus in the morning

   k) Your teacher tells you she loved your story and asks if she can read it to the class.

   l) You and another student both want the same library book, but the student lets you have it instead.

2. Have students gather in a circle and introduce the feeling dice to them. Explain to students that each side of the dice represents a different feeling. Give each student an opportunity to roll the feeling dice and talk about a time when they had that particular feeling.

Activity with Reproducible

This is a great lesson to do at the beginning of the year, especially for kindergarteners, because it introduces students to feelings, and helps them make the connection that a counselor is someone who helps students with their feelings. Distribute one activity sheet to each student and tell students you would like them to draw a face that shows how they're feeling today. Assure students that there is no right or wrong answer – they are free to draw a picture of whatever feeling they may be having.

My Feeling Face

Directions: *Draw a face that shows how you're feeling today.*

My class met with our school counselor today. We talked about feelings. This is the feeling face that I drew.

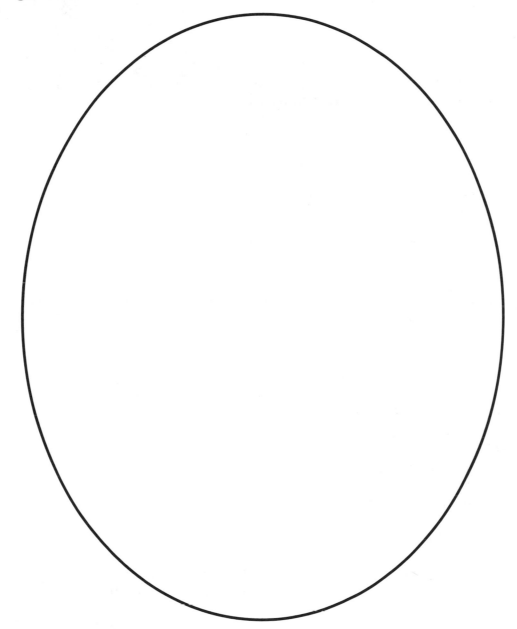

My counselor's name is _____. My counselor's

phone number is _____, and my counselor's email address

is _____.

Today I Feel Silly

Book: *Today I Feel Silly* by Jamie Lee Curtis

Publisher: HarperCollins

Grade Levels: K-2

Setting: Individual, Small Group, Classroom

Book Description

A spunky, red-headed little girl invites readers to experience the many different emotions of her week, from cranky to sad to happy. Students will be able to easily identify with the emotions in this story, and they'll love the witty rhyming verse and beautiful illustrations. This book includes an interactive feeling wheel on the last page.

Materials Needed

- **Introduction** - *one index card per student, markers*
- **Extension Activity #1** - *strips of white paper*
- **Extension Activity #2** - *a large bag of Skittles™ candy and a small container*

Preparation

- **Extension Activity #1** - *Cut the paper into enough individual strips so every student has one. Write a different feeling word on each strip of paper.*

Introduction

After greeting students, distribute an index card and a marker to each student (no yellow markers). Ask each student to write on the card in large letters one word that describes how he or she is feeling right now – be sure to let students know that you're not looking for a particular answer – this will encourage them to be more honest. When all students are finished, ask them to hold up their cards and look around at the variety of responses. Point out how rare it is for everyone to have the same feelings at the same time. Invite students to share why they wrote down the words that they did. Ask students how their feelings and moods affect the kind of day they have, and tell students you'd like to share a story with them about a girl who experiences a wide variety of feelings throughout the week.

Follow-up Questions (after reading)

1. How did the girl in the book feel at the beginning of the book? What were some of her feelings in the middle of the book? What kind of days did she have toward the end of the book?

2. Why do you think she felt so different every day? What were some of the things that happened to her that affected her feelings?

3. Do you have different feelings every day? What are some of the things that can make your feelings change?

4. Who were some of the people in the book that helped the character deal with her feelings? Who helps you with your feelings when you're not having a great day?

Extension Activities

1. Place 10-20 feeling word strips into a container. Ask for a volunteer to come to the front of the class and choose a feeling. The student should act out the feeling, using facial gestures and body language, and have the rest of the class guess the feeling. Allow enough time for every child who wants to come to the front of the room.

2. Have students gather in a circle. Give each student a small handful of Skittles™ and instruct them not to eat any yet. Tell students you're going to play the Skittles™ feeling game – each color Skittle™ will correspond to a different feeling. For instance, orange will represent happy feelings, red will represent angry feelings, yellow will represent scared feelings, green will represent sad feelings and purple will represent proud feelings (you can change these to fit your needs – and it might be helpful to make a visual chart for children so they don't have to keep asking with color goes with which feeling). Go around the circle, and have each student choose a Skittle™ from their pile and name a time when they felt the feeling the color represents. Go around the circle at least twice to make sure every child has a chance to name at least two feelings. Children can eat their Skittles™ when they're done.

Activity with Reproducible

Distribute the following activity sheet to students and ask them to draw a detailed picture of how they're feeling today, and to include the word(s) that describes their feeling. Encourage them to think of more specific feelings than "good" or "happy" if they can. Once all students have finished their drawings, allow them time to share with the class.

Today I Feel...

Yesterday I Had the Blues

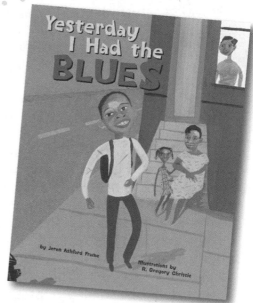

Book: *Yesterday I Had the Blues* by Jeron Ashford Frame

Publisher: Tricycle Press

Target Grades: 2-5

Setting: Individual, Small Group, Classroom

Book Description

Awarded the Ezra Jack Keats New Writer Award, this book tells the story of an African American boy that had the "blues" one day. Through the book's poetic language and vivid pictures, he discovers that his family members have different colored days too. His sister describes her day as "pink," and his grandma describes hers as "yellow." This is a wonderful multicultural book that allows children to discover how colors can evoke certain feelings. It teaches students that feelings change from day to day and stresses the importance of family and friends' support during our "blue" days!

Materials Needed

- **Extension Activity #1 -** *paint (finger paints, watercolors, etc.), large sheets of paper, paintbrushes*
- **Extension Activity #2 -** *"My Many Colored Days" by Dr. Seuss*
- **Extension Activity #3 -** *various genres of music (classical, blues, folk), crayons, drawing paper*
- **Extension Activity #4 -** *multi-colored jelly beans*

Preparation

- **Extension Activity #1 -** *Set up the classroom for painting.*

Introduction

Invite children to come to the reading area. Ask them if they have ever heard someone say that they have the "blues." Depending on children's responses, ask them what they think people mean when they use that phrase. Emphasize that certain colors tend to make us feel a particular way. Introduce the book by telling students that they will now hear a story about a boy who learned about the strong connection between feelings and colors.

Follow-up Questions (after reading)

1. Name the different colors that were represented in the book. Can you identify 2-3 feeling words you would attach to each color?

2. What do you notice about the illustrations in the book (each page follows a different color scheme)?

3. Do you ever have the "blues?" What do you do when you feel this way? How do your family and friends support you?

4. What colors are in your bedroom? Did you choose those colors? Do they make you feel a certain way?

Extension Activities

1. Provide each student or group of students with a set of paints (preferably finger paints or Tempera paints) and a large sheet of drawing paper. Ask them to think about how they are feeling today and create a picture using the color that represents that feeling. When students are finished, hang their art work on a clothing line to display. Allow all children to share their painting if they wish. Title the exhibit, "Our Many-Colored Days!"

2. Do a follow-up lesson with Dr. Seuss's book, *My Many Colored Days*.

3. Explain to students that music also has the power to evoke strong emotions. Sometimes we pick music that matches our mood. Ask students to share what type of music they like to listen to and how it makes them feel. Play different genres of music and ask students to close their eyes. What pictures come to mind? You can also provide them with paper and crayons and ask them to draw what comes to mind when they hear the different pieces of music.

4. Bring in a bag of multi-colored jelly beans. Ask students to choose the color that represents how they feel that day. Ask them to find their classmates who chose the same color and form small groups. When they are in their small groups, ask them to share with each other why they chose that particular color. Were the reasons similar or different? Remind students that there are no right and wrong answers. One color may evoke different reactions in two people.

Activity with Reproducible

Ask students to create a diamonte poem about one color. Hand out copies of the reproducible and allow students to work with a partner. Use the directions below as a guide. Note: The first reproducible can be used for a rough draft. The second reproducible should be used for the final draft.

_____
(subject)

_____
(two adjectives describing the subject)

_____
(three words ending in "ing" telling about the subject)

_____
(four words: the first two describe the subject; the last two describe its opposite)

_____
(three words ending in "ing" telling about the opposite)

_____
(two adjectives describing the opposite)

_____
(opposite)

My Color Diamonte

_____

(color)

_____

(two adjectives describing the color)

_____

(three words ending in "ing" telling about the subject)

_____

(four words: the first two words describe the subject; the last two
describe its opposite color)

_____

(three words ending in "ing" telling about the opposite color)

_____

(two adjectives that describe the opposite color)

_____

(opposite color)

My Color Diamonte

_____

_____

_____

_____

_____

_____

_____

Friendship

Learning to make and maintain friendships is crucial to children's self-esteem and well-being, and is an extremely important part of childhood. During the early childhood years, friendships revolve mostly around play. When children hit the middle-to-late elementary years, they realize that friendships have the potential to be long lasting, and they then choose their friends based on personal qualities. During middle and high school, many teens experience changing friendships, recognizing that they may not be as close with friends from their younger years.

All of these stages of friendship are natural and healthy. However, they are not always easy or without heartache. Friendship takes work, patience, and at times, a bit of courage. The books in this section can help children navigate friendship's winding path by allowing them the opportunity to connect with the book characters and learn positive friendship strategies from the realistic storylines.

Charlie the Caterpillar

Book: *Charlie the Caterpillar* by Dom Deluise

Publisher: Aladdin

Grade Levels: K-3

Setting: Individual, Group, Classroom

Book Description

Charlie the Caterpillar meets group after group of animals playing together, and he asks if he can join in. But each time he's told he is not welcome because he's ugly. As winter approaches, Charlie spins himself a cocoon. And when Charlie turns into a beautiful butterfly, everyone suddenly begs him to be part of their group. This is a great story about the meaning of true friendship.

Materials Needed

- *Introduction* - *a caterpillar puppet that turns into a butterfly, (if available) one very wrinkled and torn brown paper bag with candy inside, and one pretty gift bag filled with broken pencils, old food wrappers and/or rocks*
- *Extension Activity #1* - *a large stack of yellow and green construction paper circles, a black marker, glue stick, and one piece of poster board*
- *Extension Activity #2* - *tape, and enough different colored paper so every pair of students has one color and there are no duplicates (if you have 20 students, you'll need 10 colors of paper)*

Preparation

- *Introduction* - *Fill a wrinkled paper bag with enough wrapped candy for every student to have a piece and fill a pretty gift bag with broken pencils, old food wrappers and/or rocks.*
- *Extension Activity #1* - *Cut 20-30 circles out of yellow and green construction paper.*
- *Extension Activity #2* - *Make or copy a pattern of a large butterfly, then copy one butterfly for every pair of students in the group or class – each butterfly should be copied on a different colored paper. Cut each butterfly in half.*

Introduction

Walk into the room holding both bags. Greet students and tell them you have a gift for them, but that they can only open one bag, and you'd like them to choose which bag to open. Have students "vote" for the bag they'd all like to open by raising their hands (students will unanimously choose the pretty gift bag). When they've made their decision, make a big deal out of revealing the contents of the bag. Students will likely be very surprised – and disappointed – when you pour out the bag contents. Ask them if they'd like to see what's in the brown bag, and then slowly pour out the candy. Have students share why they chose the gift bag first, and ask why none of them chose the brown bag. Discuss the concept of "not judging a book by its cover" and stress to students that what's really important is not outward appearance, but what's on the inside – whether talking about bags or friends. Help students understand that it's important to choose our friends based on their "inside qualities" and not what they look like on the outside. Introduce students to your "friend" Charlie, who is a caterpillar puppet (if you don't have access to a caterpillar puppet, use a picture or photograph). Tell students that you're going to read a book to them about a long journey Charlie took, and you'd like them to listen carefully to see if he meets any true friends along the way.

Follow-up Questions (after reading)

1. How was Charlie feeling at the beginning of the story?

2. What were the animals like that Charlie met along the way? How did they treat him when he wanted to play? Why do you think they treated him this way?

3. Do you think Charlie's feelings were hurt by what the animals said? Why or why not?

4. Have you ever had anyone treat you the same way? How did you handle it?

5. Why did all the animals want to be Charlie's friend after he became a butterfly? Do you think this was fair? Why or why not?

6. Have you ever known anyone who was mean to you one day and nice to you the next? Is that a sign of a true friend?

7. If you were Charlie, do you think you would have played with the animals the second time around?

8. How did Charlie show he was a real friend at the end of the story?

Extension Activities

1. As a class, have students brainstorm different things they could say or do to be a real friend. Write their ideas on the board or on a piece of chart paper. After students have come up with enough ideas, give each student a green or yellow circle and ask them to write or draw their idea on the circle. If students would like to do more than one circle, let them do so. When all students have finished, have each student share their circle with the class and then let them glue it on a blank piece of poster board (or the classroom wall/bulletin board) to make a friendship caterpillar. After the body of the caterpillar is complete, students can have fun adding details like feet, eyes, antennas, etc. Students can continue to add to the friendship caterpillar throughout the year as they learn additional ways to be a real friend. Some caterpillars make it all the way around the room! **Variation: Depending on the size of your group, you might want to divide students into smaller groups and have each group make their own caterpillar – this could also be an individual student project that students could take home with them when finished.

2. Distribute half of a butterfly to each student and tell students you'd like them to each find the person who has the other half of their butterfly. Once students have found their butterfly partner, tell them you'd like them each to write one way that they are a good friend on their half of the butterfly, but you would like them to work together to come up with a design for their butterfly that will match (look symmetrical) when they put it together. Remind students how important it is for us to listen to others, and how friends work together to come up with ideas, rather than bossing each other around. After students have each written their friend quality on the butterfly, ask them to share it with their butterfly partner before moving on to the design. When students have finished, they may tape their butterflies together. When all butterflies are complete, allow all pairs to "introduce" their butterfly to the class. Talk about how all the butterflies are unique because they all have two different friendship qualities, and how they are all beautiful because people worked together to create them.

Activity with Reproducible

Review with students that a true friend values us for who we are on the inside, and for the good things we do, not what we look like on the outside. Unless you have already done Extension Activity #1 with students, give them a few minutes to brainstorm, as a class, some qualities of a true friend. Tell students you'd like them to complete the following activity sheet by drawing a picture of themselves in the center and then drawing and writing one way that they're a good friend in each of the two remaining blank squares. Encourage students to think of other things to write and draw besides, "I am nice," which is usually the most common characteristic children think of.

I am a good friend because...

THIS IS ME

How to Lose All Your Friends

Book: *How to Lose all your Friends* by Nancy Carlson

Publisher: Puffin

Grade Levels: 2-4

Setting: Individual, Small Group, Classroom

Book Description

This vividly illustrated book uses humor to clearly communicate common things children do to hurt, upset or annoy other children. While written as a "guide book" to illustrate the many surefire ways children can *lose* friends, children will clearly understand the difference between good and bad friend behavior, and by hearing what *not* to do, they will internalize what they *should* do to make and keep friends.

Materials Needed

- ***Extension Activity #1 -*** *one sheet of white bulletin board paper per student, crayons or markers*
- ***Extension Activity #2 -*** *several large sheets of white chart paper/bulletin board paper*

Preparation: None needed

Introduction

Ask the students to think about some of their friends, and to think about why they like those friends. Have students name some qualities of a good friend and write their ideas on the board. Allow some time for students to share stories about when they were a good friend to someone else, and when someone else was a good friend to them. Write down all ideas. Make the point that in order to make and keep friends, you have to be a good friend yourself. Tell students you would like to share a funny book with them that gives advice for what to do if you **don't** want to have any friends.

Follow-up Questions (after reading)

1. The book talked about six different ways we can lose our friends. Who can name some of the ways?

2. How many of you have had problems with someone else not sharing? Bullying you? Being a poor sport? Tattling on you? Whining? What did it feel like when people did these things to you?

3. How many of you have ever acted like the girl in the book who doesn't have friends? Of all the things the book listed, are any especially hard for you to **not** do? Which ones, and why?

4. Can you think of six different ways you could **make** friends?

5. What did the girl in the book do at the end that made her a better friend?

Extension Activities

1. Tell students they will be making their own class book – "How to Make Friends." Divide the class into six small groups. Assign each group a topic/chapter from the book and have them turn it into a positive (ex. Never share/Share). Give each student in each group a piece of white drawing paper. Their job is to think about their topic, then choose one example from the list they came up with earlier that fits under that topic, and illustrate a picture to match the phrase – so depending on how many students are in the group, each group will come up with 4-6 illustrations and explanations that match their category. Once all students are finished, ask for volunteers to share their drawings with the class. When everyone is completely done, collect the pages and bind them together in a book for the class to keep. Tell students that whenever they're having trouble making or keeping friends, they can go to the class book for helpful reminders and examples.

2. Tell students that they're going to have some "new students" join their class and that you know they're all going to be great friends – because they'll be creating the new students themselves. Divide students into small groups and give a handful of markers and a large piece of bulletin board paper to each group. Have students choose one person in their group to lie down on the paper while the other students use markers to trace the outline of his/her body (no girls in skirts!). Once each group has completed their outline, have them name the "new student" and work together to come up with qualities and characteristics that would make the new student a perfect friend. Ask students to list these qualities and characteristics on the part of the body it would correspond to, if applicable (for example, if they think being kind or caring is important, have them write this where the heart would be, being smart would be written near the brain, etc.) Once students have exhausted all possible good friend qualities, allow them to add details to their new friend, such as hair color, eye color, and clothing. When all students are finished, have each group introduce their new friend to the class. Students have a great time with this activity!

Activity with Reproducible

Distribute the following activity sheet to students and tell them you'd like them to use what they learned from the book and turn bad friends into good friends by unscrambling the friendship characteristics.

Turn Bad Friends into Good Friends...

Directions: *The left side of the page lists some qualities we would not want our friends to have. Turn these qualities into good friendship qualities by filling in the blanks. Then unscramble the circled letters to find out what kind of new friend you have.*

Lying   ___ ___ N E ___ (T)

Angry   H (◯) P ___ ___

Frowning   S ___ ___ L ___ ___ (G)

Selfish   S ___ A (R) ___ ___ G

Rude   ___ O L ___ T (◯)

Mean   K ___ ___ D

What kind of new friend do you have?

_____ _____ _____ _____ _____

Sorry!

Book: *Sorry* by Trudy Ludwig

Publisher: Tricycle Press

Target Grades: 2-5

Setting: Individual, Group, Classroom

Book Description

Jack was one of the most unpopular kids in school. However, one day he rescued Charlie's Frisbee from a rooftop and gained his approval. Although Jack is infatuated with his instant popularity, he does not always like how Charlie treats other people. Whether he is drawing mustaches on his sister's pictures or pressuring Jack to throw water balloons at unsuspecting neighbors, Charlie believes that an insincere apology can right all of his wrongs. After the boys ruin a classmate's science fair project, Charlie learns that "I'm sorry" doesn't always "cut it." The science teacher teaches them that a sincere apology includes actions as well as words. The book includes discussion questions and a chart that lists the "do's and don'ts" of a genuine apology.

Materials Needed

- *Extension Activity #1 -* *10-15 index cards with feeling words on each card, chart paper or whiteboard, drawing paper, crayons or markers*
- *Activity with Reproducible - pencils*

Preparation

- *Extension Activity #1 - Write various feeling words on 10-15 index cards. Make sure they are feeling words that can be easily acted out during a game of Charades.*

Introduction

Ask students if they have ever given an apology to a friend or family member. If they are honest, they should all raise their hands! Next, ask them if they have ever been forced to apologize to someone when they were not actually sorry. Ask them to give examples. Explain to them that they will be listening to a story about a boy who learned the importance of a sincere apology.

Follow-up Questions (after reading)

1. What makes a good (sincere) apology different from a bad (insincere) apology? (Write the students' answers on the board or on a large piece of chart paper)

2. How did Jack know that Charlie's apologies were insincere? Are you able to tell when someone's apology is insincere?

3. Have you ever been forced to give an apology when you weren't ready? How did you feel?

4. What made Jack continue to be friends with Charlie? Have you ever made a bad choice because you were afraid to lose a friend?

5. Do you think Leena forgave Jack too quickly? How would you have handled this situation if you were Leena?

6. Do you think that Charlie learned a lesson at the end of the book? What clues lead you to this conclusion?

Extension Activities

1. One aspect of Charlie's insincere apology was his poor body language. Introduce the topic of body language and the important role it plays in communication. Ask for two student volunteers to demonstrate the power of body language. Ask the first student to say the sentence, "Are you coming?" with an annoyed body stance. Ask the second student to say the same sentence in an excited manner. Talk about the two very different messages that they send to their recipient. Play a short game of feelings charades to focus on body language. Write 10-15 feeling words on index cards and have one student act out the feeling without using any words. The first student to guess the feeling has the option of being the next actor or actress. Play until each student has had an opportunity to act out a feeling.

2. There is a mini-lesson on popularity and peer pressure within the book. Until the end of the book, Charlie makes a lot of his poor choices out of fear of becoming unpopular again. Ask students what makes students popular at their school. Is it someone's appearance? Is it their character? Is it their abilities? As an additional activity, divide students into pairs and ask them to draw a picture of what makes a boy or girl popular at school. Come back as a group to discuss the drawings.

Activity with Reproducible

Using the reproducible, ask students to write an apology letter to Leena from Jack, including the essential components of a good apology. Refer to the discussion guide at the back of the book. Have students share their letters with the group when they are finished.

"I'm Sorry..."

Directions: *Write an apology letter to Leena from Jack. Remember to include all of the parts of a good (sincere) apology. You may use the book as a guide.*

Dear Leena,

_____

_____

_____

_____

_____

_____

_____

_____

Your friend,
Jack

What's the Recipe for Friends?

Book: *What's The Recipe For Friends?* by Greg Williamson

Publisher: Peerless Publishing

Grade Levels: 1-3

Setting: Small Group or Classroom

Book Description

When Freddy and his family move to a new town, he is worried that he won't make any new friends. His mom tells him that she has a special recipe for making friends, and she shares it with him. Freddy uses all of his "ingredients" during his first few days of school, and although it takes a little patience, the "recipe" finally works.

Materials Needed

- *Extension Activity #1 - chef's hat, apron, a big bowl, a large wooden spoon, 4 empty film canisters labeled: kindness, politeness, sharing, and taking turns, a poster board with a cut-out of a black pot glued to the bottom half, and a stack of 3x5 cards cut from brightly colored construction paper (or use colored index cards)*
- *Extension Activity #2 - one piece of drawing paper for each student*

Preparation

- *Extension Activity #1 - Get 4 empty film canisters (or another small cylindrical container) and label them kindness, politeness, sharing and taking turns. Cut a large black pot out of construction paper and glue it to the bottom of a piece of poster board, cut a stack of 3x5 cards out of various colored construction paper.*

Introduction

Walk into the room wearing your chef's hat and apron, and carrying a big bowl and large spoon. Ask students if they have any idea why you're dressed the way you are. Once they mention cooking or baking, ask them if there are any other tools we need – other than kitchen appliances – to help us cook. Once they've mentioned that we usually need a recipe to tell us how to cook something, ask if any of them have ever used a recipe to help someone cook. Discuss the fact that a recipe contains a list of important ingredients needed to make the food. Explain to students that today they're going to read a book that will teach them part of the recipe for friends, then they will work together to come up with the rest of the ingredients needed for making friends.

Follow Up Questions

1. What was Freddy worried about in the beginning of the story? Have you ever been new to a school and worried that you wouldn't make friends?

2. If you have felt like Freddy before, did you share your worries with anyone?

3. What were the four main ingredients Freddy's mom told him about? Can you think of a time when you have demonstrated those ingredients to someone else? What about a time when someone else has demonstrated those ingredients for you?

4. Why do you think it took a few days for the ingredients to really work? Do you think Freddy felt like giving up? How do you think you might have felt if you were Freddy?

5. What other ingredients do you think are important for making new friends? Can you share a time when you've used one of those ingredients to be a good friend?

Extension Activities

1. Tell the students you're going to see if, as a group, you can make Freddy's recipe work. While wearing your chef's hat and apron, open each "spice container" and pretend to stir the four spices in the bowl. Every few seconds, stop to show them the empty bowl, and ask them if they think you've cooked up some friendship yet. They get a kick out of this if you ham it up. After they agree that nothing is happening, ask if they can make the recipe better by using some of the ideas they thought of earlier. Put the stack of "recipe cards" in the middle of the table and have students write as many friendship ingredients as they can think of on the cards (one idea/ingredient per card). Ask the students to toss their recipe cards in the bowl as they finish each one. Continue stirring the "ingredients" with your spoon until the students are done with ideas. Then, have each student draw a card out of the bowl, read the ingredient listed, and then glue it right above the pot. When all the cards have been placed on the poster board, the class will have their own Recipe for Friends.

2. Ask students how many of them have ever been new to a school, and give those students an opportunity to share how it felt to be "the new kid." Talk with all students about the challenges of being new to a school, and having to make all new friends. Tell students they will be making a class book to help make things easier for new students who may join their class. Hand out a piece of drawing paper to each student and tell students you'd like them to draw a picture of themselves and underneath the picture you'd like them to list three or four things they would like a new student to know about them – preferably three or four things that make them a good friend. When everyone has completed their page, you can make a class book out of it by using inexpensive plastic binding for the edges. Whenever new students come, they can look through the book to learn more about everyone in their class.

Activity With Reproducible

Now that students are familiar with the many qualities that make up a good friend, tell them you'd like them to search for these qualities in others. To give them some practice "searching," distribute the following word find and ask students to try and find all of the qualities hidden in the word search. Tell students the words may be listed horizontal, vertical or diagonal – but not backwards!

Friendship Word Find

```
G J B O A S E T O
T P M Y N C S T F
M C A R I N G N R
K H O N E S T P I
I V K T T P V D E
N T S I A D E A N
D I F U N N Y O D
L M P O L I T E L
L O Y A L D X R Y
T S H A R E S W T
```

WORD BANK

Kind	Honest	Nice	Loyal	Funny
Listens	Caring	Shares	Polite	Friendly

Goal-Setting and Persevering

Whether children are learning to tie their shoes or embarking on long division, each developmental stage requires perseverance and the ability to work toward goals. Teaching children to keep trying, in spite of obstacles they might face along the way, is an important lesson. Children who persevere are typically more creative problem solvers, more patient, and have less anxiety and lower frustration levels than children who give up easily. Learning to set goals and then reach those goals, helps children gain a sense of accomplishment and build a sense of self.

In this section you will meet a child who takes a walk in the rain with a brain, a small train that learns the power of positive thinking, a real-life athlete who overcame great odds to achieve her goal, and a girl who learns that winning isn't always the most important thing. Use these books to inspire, teach and entertain children. Adults may find themselves re-inspired as well!

A Walk in the Rain with a Brain

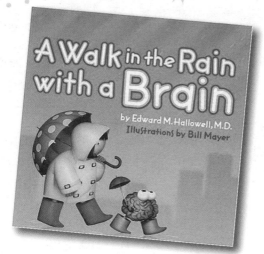

Book: *A Wak in the Rain with a Brain* by Dr. Edward Hallowell

Publisher: HarperCollins

Grade Levels: K-2

Setting: Individual, Group, Classroom

Book Description

In this whimsical tale, we meet Lucy, a young girl out for a walk in the rain. Along the way, Lucy runs into a brain, named Fred, who is looking for his missing head. As Fred and Lucy try to locate his head, she asks him if he can help make her smart. Fred tells her that a long time ago, all brains were treated the same, until a mean but powerful brain, named Complain, decided that some brains were better than others. Through his colorful story and poetic language, Fred teaches Lucy that all brains are smart. It is everyone's job to nurture their brain and "feed" it many different activities. By doing this, we discover what our brain likes best. This is a wonderful book for the start of a new school year.

Materials Needed

* *Introduction* - *model or picture of a human brain*
* *Extension Activity #1* - *"Brain Day" materials (board games, healthy snacks, music)*
* *Activity with Reproducible* - *crayons or markers*

Preparation

* *Extension Activity #1* - *Talk to the teacher about hosting a Brain Day.*

Introduction

Show students a model or picture of the human brain. Ask them to guess what it is. After they have guessed the correct answer, share with them several fun brain facts including: (A) the brain is a muscle (B) your brain is the boss of your body and (C) the average brain weighs approximately 3 pounds. Explain that you are going to read a silly book about a girl named Lucy and a brain named Fred. Tell students that even though it is a make-believe story, there is an important message about our very special brains.

Follow-up Questions (after reading)

1. How is Lucy feeling when she first meets Fred? What made her feel this way?

2. Describe the character Complain. What made him decide that some brains are smarter than others?

3. How was Lucy feeling by the end of the book? What made her feel this way?

4. What does your brain like to do?

5. How can we take care of our brains so that they grow and develop?

6. Are there any new activities that your brain would like to try?

Extension Activities

1. Building on follow-up question #5, explain that the human brain is a muscle. Ask them what people do to get strong muscles? To get strong muscles, people eat healthy food and exercise. In order to have a strong brain, we have to feed it healthy food and give it exercise. How do we exercise our brain? We exercise our brain by reading, playing sports, listening to music, playing games and getting enough sleep. Host a "Brain Day" where the students eat a healthy snack, such as fruit and pretzels, and play brain games such as Scrabble Junior™ or Sequence for Kids™.

2. Play Brain Charades by asking each student to think of one activity that their brain enjoys. One at a time, allow each student to act out the activity without saying any words. Have the other students guess the activity.

Activity with Reproducible

Hand out the activity sheet and crayons to each student. Show them the outline of the brain that is divided into four sections. Ask them to think about four activities their brain likes to do. Instruct them to draw one activity in each section of the brain. When the students are finished, give them an opportunity to share "their brains" with the group.

A Walk in the Rain with My Brain!

Directions: In each of the four brain sections, draw one activity that your brain likes to do. These activities can include sports, music, school subjects or other hobbies.

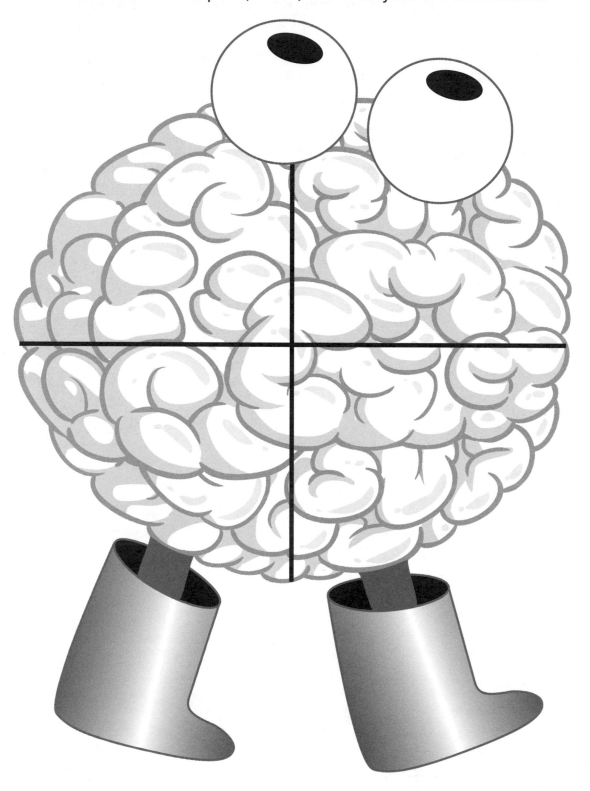

Name _____

The Little Engine That Could

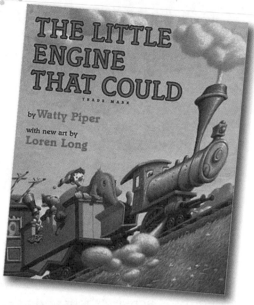

Book: *The Little Engine That Could* by Watty Piper

Publisher: Penguin USA

Grade Levels: 2-5

Setting: Individual, Group, Classroom

Book Description

This classic story introduces us to a little train who is determined to make it to the other side of the mountain to deliver its goods. Repeating the infamous phrase, "I Think I Can" and finding encouragement from his friend, the little train finally reaches his goal. This story is ideal for developing goals at the beginning of the school year, creating New Year's resolutions, or brainstorming goals for the first session of a small group.

Materials Needed

- ***Extension Activity #1 -*** *sticky notes (Post-It™ Notes)*

Preparation: None

Introduction

Write the word *goal* on the board. Ask students to come up with their own definition of the word to share with the group. After gathering definitions, tell students that you are going to share a book they're probably all familiar with. Ask them to listen to the story and consider which character works hard toward his or her goal.

Follow-up Questions (after reading)

1. What was the engine's goal?

2. Why didn't the other engines stop to help the toys?

3. Who helped the engine reach his goal? How did they help him?

4. Have you ever faced a difficult challenge? What did you do? Did anyone support you as you worked toward your goal?

5. Do you ever "talk yourself through" a tough situation (maybe a hard class at school)? What do you say to motivate yourself?

Extension Activities

1. Speak with the students about personal, social and academic goals. Give each student three sticky notes and ask them to write one goal for each category. Instruct them to put the sticky notes somewhere they will see them often, such as a daily planner or their locker. Periodically check in with students to see if they are still on track with their goals. If not, what has happened? How can they get back on track?

2. Ask students to think about someone they know that "beat the odds" and reached their goal, particularly when no one believed that they could achieve it. For example, Michael Jordan was a professional basketball player, but was cut from his high school basketball team. Rosa Parks was an African American woman who fought segregation. Albert Einstein became a famous scientist despite his dyslexia. Talk about the qualities these individuals possessed that helped them reach their goals.

Activity with Reproducible

Lead a discussion about realistic versus unrealistic goals. What makes a goal realistic? What makes a goal unrealistic? Ask students to think about what might happen if they make unrealistic goals. Have each student identify one realistic goal they can make and who they can count on to be their Support Buddy. Hand out the activity sheet and ask them to complete it. When they are finished, ask them to share their goal with the group (if the activity is being done in a small group) or a partner (if the activity is being done in the class).

I Think I Can, I Think I Can

Directions: After listening to the story, make one realistic goal for yourself. Answer the questions below to help you think through your plan for achieving your goal.

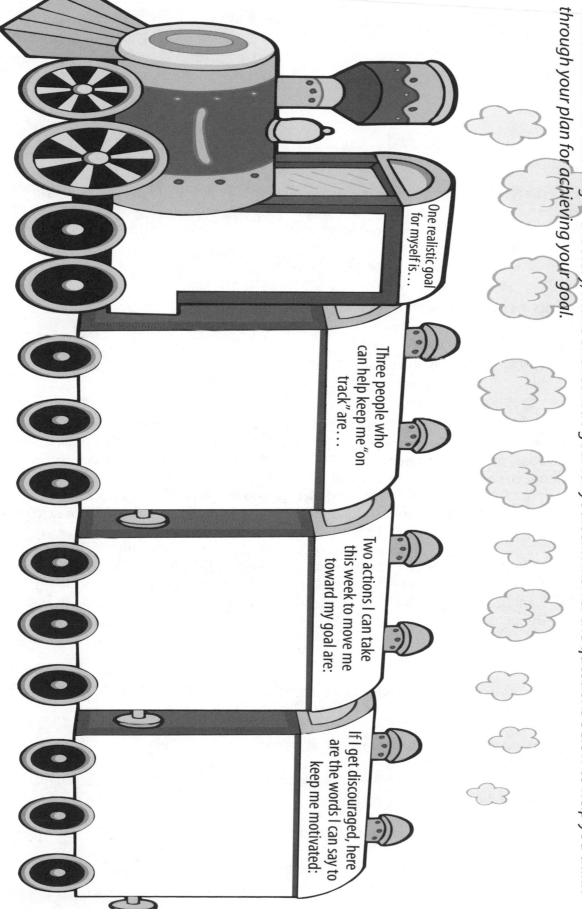

One realistic goal for myself is…

Three people who can help keep me "on track" are…

Two actions I can take this week to move me toward my goal are:

If I get discouraged, here are the words I can say to keep me motivated:

Wilma Unlimited

Book: *Wilma Unlimited* by Nadjmeh Salimi

Publisher: Sandpiper

Grade Levels: 3-5

Setting: Individual, Small Group, Classroom

Book Description

This beautifully illustrated book tells the triumphant and inspiring true story of runner Wilma Rudolph, who overcame childhood polio and eventually went on to win three gold medals in track in a single Olympics.

Materials Needed

- *Extension Activity #2 - basketball, masking tape, permanent marker*

Preparation

- *Extension Activity #2 - You can choose to label and mark off the lines ahead of time if you'd like.*

Introduction

Discuss the meaning of perseverance with students. Make students aware that each of them has had experience with perseverance in their lives – whether it was learning to ride a bike without falling, learning to walk, learning to read, or making good grades. Discuss with students why it's important to set goals for the future, and to focus on what they **can** do, not what they can't do. Explain to students that setting goals is like having a road map. If you're headed somewhere you've never been – a new place or simply a new direction – you might not reach your destination without a road map. In the same way, you can't reach your goals unless you know what –and where – your goals are. To introduce the story, ask students to think about athletes who win Olympic Gold Medals. Make the point that those athletes worked toward the ultimate goal of a gold medal for years – they didn't simply decide to "go for the gold" while at the Olympics. Successful people – just like Olympic athletes – don't become successful by accident, but by planning what they want to achieve, working toward it every day, and by recognizing problems that might get in the way and coming up with solutions.

Follow-up Questions (after reading)

1. What were some of the physical obstacles Wilma faced in her childhood? What were some of the emotional obstacles she faced?

2. How did Wilma deal with all her problems? (she didn't give up, leg exercises)

3. What was Wilma's first huge accomplishment? (walking into the church) How do you think she felt about herself when she walked without her brace?

4. What happened to Wilma eight years after she got rid of her leg brace?

5. What helped Wilma pull ahead on her last race of the Olympics?

6. What personal characteristics did Wilma have that helped her become so successful?

7. How much did Wilma's confidence and independence play a part in her accomplishing her goals?

Extension Activities

1. Ask each student to take out a piece of notebook paper and to write down three things about themselves that they're proud of, and three goals they have for themselves this school year…three things they'd like to work toward. After they have finished their letters, hand each student an envelope and have them address the letter to themselves. Tell students you will hold onto their letters until the end of the school year, and then you will mail the letters to them. Students love looking forward to getting their letters, and they often work harder toward reaching their goals when they feel like they're held more accountable.

2. Take students to your school's basketball goal. Use masking tape to mark off lines in three different areas - the first line will be as far away as possible from the goal, (label this one D.O.) the second line should be the three point line, (label this one H.S.G.) and the third line should be marked very close to the goal (label this one C.G.) Ask for one student volunteer to stand at each of the three lines, and have each student take a turn shooting the ball from where they stand. Then have students rotate so that all three students have had a chance to shoot from all three lines. It should quickly become obvious to students that it's much harder to "make the goal" when they are furthest from it, and that it's easiest to "make the goal" when they are closest. Ask students how they think the basketball analogy relates to doing well in school then reveal what the initials on the line stand for: College Graduate, High School Graduate and Drop Out.

Activity with Reproducible

Discuss with students the key "ingredients" for setting goals. Goals should be specific, realistic, and measurable. As students are setting a goal in their mind, it helps for them to form a vivid mental picture of themselves achieving the goal. Help students understand that we don't reach our goals without many steps along the way. Tell students that completing the following activity sheet will help them visualize the important steps they'll need to take to reach their goal. Ask students to write one goal they have for themselves at the top of the activity sheet. Inside the "bronze medal" they will write the first step they'll need to take to reach their goal. Inside the "silver medal" they will write the second step they'll need to take. Inside the "gold medal" ask students to write a description of how they will know when they've reached their goal. Tell students you'd like them to keep their goal sheet somewhere they'll see it every day, so that they can keep track of the dates when they attain each of their medals.

Going for the Gold!

My Goal is: _____

I would like to reach my goal by this date: _____.

Date I received the
Bronze Medal:

_____

Date I received the
Silver Medal:

_____

Date I received the Gold Medal: _____

Winners Never Quit!

Book: *Winners Never Quit!* by Mia Hamm

Publisher: Scholastic, Inc.

Grade Levels: 1-4

Setting: Individual, Small Group, Classroom

Book Description

This autobiographical story by Olympic soccer champion Mia Hamm is a great motivator for all children. Mia loves playing soccer more than anything – until she has a bad game one day and can't score a goal. Frustrated and angry, she chooses to quit instead of losing. Her siblings are so irritated by Mia's attitude that they refuse to let her play with them anymore. It doesn't take long for Mia to realize that playing the game is more important to her than winning or losing.

Materials Needed

- *Extension Activity #1 - chart paper, a marker*
- *Extension Activity #2 - a soccer ball*

Preparation: None needed

Introduction

Ask students to raise their hands if they've ever quit something – and allow them time to share what they quit and how they felt after they quit. Ask students if any of them have ever had a time when they felt like quitting, but decided to "stick to it." Help students understand that it takes a lot more courage to stick with something, even though it might not be easy. Discuss with students that sometimes we quit something because we feel like we're not very good at it, and sometimes we quit because we *are* really good at something and can't stand the thought of failing at it, so we quit before we have a chance to fail. Tell students you'd like to share a story with them – written by an Olympic soccer champion – about a girl who quits because she hates the thought of losing so much.

Follow-up Questions (after reading)

1. What happened to Mia in the beginning of the book that made her so upset?

2. What did she do next? Why? Have you ever quit something because you hated losing?

3. Why wouldn't Mia's brothers and sisters let her play soccer the next day? How do you think Mia felt as she watched everyone else play?

4. When Mia's brother let her play again, did she get the goal? Did it bother her?

5. What did Mia realize about herself that changed her attitude?

6. Do you think quitting is easier or harder than "sticking to it?" Why?

Extension Activities

1. Discuss with students that when we quit something, we don't give ourselves a chance to get better at it – and that giving up doesn't get us any closer to reaching our goals. Instead, quitting just ends up making us feel worse about ourselves because we never learn how good we might have been at something. Tell students that sometimes the support and encouragement of our family, friends, classmates and teachers can "cheer us on" and motivate us to keep trying even when we feel like giving up. Ask students to raise their hands if they have ever gotten words of support and encouragement from someone that inspired them to keep trying – and ask them to share what those words were. As students share their experiences, write their encouraging words and phrases on a piece of chart paper. Then ask every student to brainstorm a list of supportive and encouraging words or phrases they can tell themselves – or others – to keep their spirits up and prevent them from quitting.

2. Ask students to sit in a circle in the reading area. Remind students that two common reasons people often quit is because they don't feel they're good enough at something, and they're afraid to try harder, or because – like Mia – they're really good at a particular thing and get frustrated if they mess up the thing they're good at. Hand a soccer ball to the student closest to you and ask the student to name one thing they're good at – that's easy for them – and one thing they're not good at – that they have to try harder on. Have students pass the ball around so everyone has a chance to talk. Help students understand the importance of "sticking to it" with things they're already good at – so they can build skills and confidence - as well as things they're not good at – so they can get better.

Activity with Reproducible

Discuss with students how scoring a goal in soccer is a lot like reaching a goal in life – you have to work toward it and try your best – and sometimes you have to try again and again until you make it. Explain to students that goals can be short-term or long-term, and they can be small goals or big goals. It might help to point out to students that – although not specifically mentioned as a goal in the book – one goal Mia obviously set for herself was to keep playing soccer and to not quit again just because she didn't win every time. Help students understand that reaching our goals doesn't happen automatically – we have to take small steps along the way to get there. Share with students a personal goal that you have – or a goal that you've had in the past – and tell them the steps you took to reach your goal. Ask students to share examples of goals they might have for themselves – they can be related to school or home. After several students have had a chance to respond, brainstorm a list of other possible goals that might be applicable to their grade level. Distribute the following activity sheet to students. Tell students you would like for them to come up with one goal they can work toward, and then list two things they can do to reach their goal – and finally, draw a picture of themselves reaching their goal.

I Can Reach My Goal!

Directions: *Write a goal you have for yourself on the line at the top of the page. Next, write two things you can do to reach your goal. Then draw and color a picture of you reaching your goal.*

My Goal Is: _____

_____

Two things I can do to reach my goal are:

1. _____

2. _____

Here is a picture of me reaching my goal:

Honesty

Although honesty is a character trait that comes more easily to some children than others, fortunately, it's also a skill that can be taught. One of the most important factors for teaching children honesty is having strong role models who consistently model honest behavior and expectations. These role models may be teachers, parents or other students. Although few children escape their elementary school years without telling a lie, the majority of children don't lie to be deceitful as much as they lie to avoid getting in trouble. It is important to stress to children that telling the truth will never get them in as much trouble as being caught in a lie. The books in this section address the positive consequences that can arise from being honest, as well as the negative consequences that can arise from being dishonest. Children will also learn how harmful lying can be to friendship and building trust.

Edwurd Fudwupper Fibbed Big

Book: *Edwurd Fudwupper Fibbed Big* by Berkely Breathed

Publisher: Little, Brown Young Readers

Grade Levels: 2-5

Setting: Individual, Group, Classroom

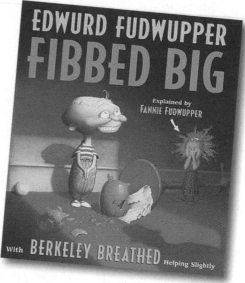

Book Description

There is no bigger fibber than Edwurd Fudwupper. He boasts to his friends that his little sister was born from a poodle. He tells plump Mabel Dill that she has been crowned queen of Brazil! However, after he breaks his mother's prized glass pig, he tells the biggest whopper of all. When his make-believe story of alien pigs and spaceships spirals out of control, Edwurd learns an important lesson about telling the truth. The book is narrated by his little sister, Fannie, who so desperately wants her older brother's attention that she takes the blame for Edwurd's tall tales.

Materials Needed

- ***Extension Activity #1*** - *a ball of string*
- ***Activity with Reproducible*** - *"Honest" and "Dishonest" signs*

Preparation

- ***Activity with Reproducible*** - *Cut apart the scenario strips. Hang the "Honest" and "Dishonest" signs on opposite sides of the classroom*

Introduction

Ask students if they have ever heard of a "fib." Gather responses. Ask if they have ever heard of any other words for "lie." Tell students that they are going to hear a story about a boy who tells a big lie and learns an important lesson. Stress that the book has a lot of humor, so while you want them to enjoy it, you also want them to listen carefully so they do not miss the story's true message.

Follow-up Questions (after reading)

1. What do you think makes Edwurd Fudwupper tell so many fibs?

2. Would you say that Edwurd has a good imagination? Do you think he is using his imagination as a strength or a weakness?

3. How do you think Fannie feels about her brother, Edwurd?

4. What made Fannie take the blame for breaking the glass pig when she did not really do it? Have you ever taken the blame for something that you did not do?

5. Have you ever heard of the saying, "A web of lies?" What do you think this means? How did Edwurd get caught up in a web of lies?

Extension Activities

1. To build on follow-up question #5, demonstrate the concept of a "web of lies." Ask the students to stand up and create a circle. Explain that you will be starting the "lie" with one open-ended sentence (think of a common lie that students could relate to). You will then toss a ball of string to someone in the circle, while still holding on to the loose end of the string. That person should build onto your lie, by continuing the story with another lie and tossing the ball of string to another student. Continue the pattern until everyone has added to the story. Ask students to look at the complicated web of string. What would they have to do to wind up the string and get it back into a nice, neat ball of string. How is this similar to what happens when someone tells a lie to a friend?

2. To build on follow-up question #2, lead a discussion about Edwurd's wonderful imagination. In the story, his imagination was leading him to tell some big whoppers! Brainstorm several ways that Edwurd could use his imagination in a positive way. Ask students if they have ever turned one of their weaknesses into a strength.

Activity with Reproducible

Cut apart the scenario strips and copy the "honest" and "dishonest" signs. Hang up the signs on opposite sides of the classroom. Divide students into pairs and give each pair one of the strips. Ask them to read the scenario with their partner and decide whether it is an honest or dishonest situation. Tell them to move to the side of the room that represents their choice. After all students have chosen a side, read the strips and ask students if they agree or disagree with their classmates.

HONEST

DISHONEST

Honest or Dishonest Scenarios

You lost a video game that a friend loaned you, but you tell them that it was stolen.

You see another student copying the answers during a spelling test, but you keep your eyes on your paper only.

The class pet gets out of the cage while you were watching it, but you tell the teacher that someone else let it out.

You are shopping with your parents and see a lady drop a dollar bill. You pick it up and give it back to her.

You borrow some crayons from a friend and accidentally break one of them. You return them to your friend, but don't say anything about one of them being broken.

You tell your parents why you were late even though you know you will be in trouble.

You tell your teacher that you returned a library book when you can't really remember if you did or not.

A friend asks you if you want to go see a scary movie with him. Although you really want him to like you, you say that you do not like scary movies because they give you bad dreams. You offer to watch another movie with him instead of the scary one.

You know that it isn't your turn to choose the game in PE because you went last week. Everyone else thinks that it is your turn though, so you decide not to correct them.

Liar, Liar, Pants on Fire

Book: *Liar, Liar, Pants on Fire* by Miriam Cohen

Publisher: Starbright Books

Grade Levels: K-2

Setting: Individual, Group, Classroom

Book Description

When the new first grader, Alex, brags about having a pony and a triple rocket launcher, his classmates call him a liar. This leads to his classmates teasing him and excluding him from group games. When their teacher asks them to put themselves in Alex's shoes, she reminds them that it is not easy being the new student. When Alex helps a classmate in need, the students see him in a new light and decide to give him a second chance. By doing this, Alex learns that lying is not the best way to get attention and make friends.

Materials Needed

- ***Extension Activity #2*** - *large chart paper, white drawing paper, crayons or markers*
- ***Activity with Reproducible*** - *pencils*

Preparation: None needed

Introduction

Invite students to the reading area. Ask them if they are familiar with the definition of a *lie*. Connect their definition with the word *honesty*. Show them the book cover and explain that they are going to hear a story about a little boy who got into a habit of lying. Ask students to listen carefully to the story to see if they can discover how the boy was feeling right before he told the lies and how his classmates felt about his dishonesty.

Follow-up Questions (after reading)

1. Why did Alex lie about having a pony and a triple rocket launcher? How do you think he was feeling?

2. How did the other students respond to him? How were they feeling?

3. What happened at the holiday party that changed the students' opinions about Alex?

4. Have you ever been the new student in the classroom? How did it feel?

5. What lesson(s) did Alex learn about making friends?

Extension Activities

1. One reason Alex may have lied is because he could not think of any better ways to start a conversation with his classmates. Ask students to name feelings they have when they meet someone new. Sometimes these feelings make us uneasy. Brainstorm various "sentence starters," sentences they can use when they meet someone new. Examples could include, "What games do you like to play?" or "I like your shoes. Blue is one of my favorite colors." Role-play these "sentence starters" as a group.

2. One of the underlying messages of this book is that it can be very difficult to be the new student in a classroom. At one point in the story, the first graders were too busy playing to help Alex learn the routine of the classroom. Tell students that they are going to make a classroom handbook that includes many of the daily classroom routines. This handbook can then be given to any new student that enters the classroom during the year. They should include restroom procedures, Show and Tell rules, classroom reward systems etc. Brainstorm ideas on the board or large chart paper. Divide the routines among the students and ask them to write and illustrate their designated page. Collect the students' papers, bind them together and present the handbook as a welcoming gift to new students.

Activity with Reproducible

Hand out the honesty maze and allow students to work in pairs.

Liar, Liar, Pants on Fire

Directions: *Sometimes being a new student feels like you are in a maze. Help Alex, the new student, get through the maze. Note the story words within the maze.*

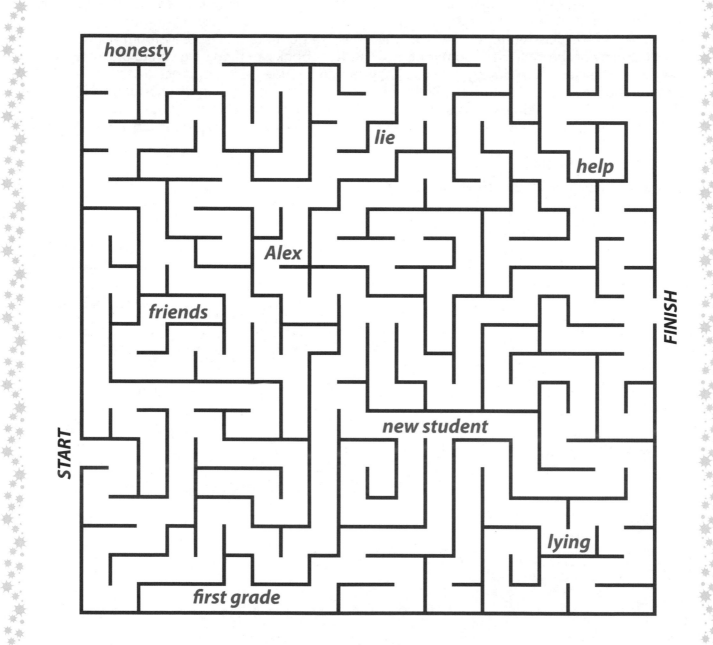

Name _____

© YouthLight, Inc.

The Empty Pot

Book: *The Empty Pot* by Demi

Publisher: Henry Holt and Co.

Grade Levels: 2-5

Setting: Individual, Small Group, Classroom

Book Description

When Ping admits that he is the only child in China who is unable to grow a flower from the seeds distributed by the Emperor, he is rewarded for his honesty by being crowned the next Emperor. Students love the surprise ending to this old Chinese folktale.

Materials Needed

- *Extension Activity #1* - *packets of flower or vegetable seeds, small paper or plastic cups, potting soil, strips of paper long enough to encircle the small paper cup, scotch tape*
- *Extension Activity #2* - *a ball of yarn*

Preparation

- *Extension Activity #2* - *Select a student ahead of time and prep that student for the activity.*
- *Activity with Reproducible* - *Copy the scenarios and cut them into strips ahead of time.*

Introduction

Have students join you in the reading area, and ask them several of the following questions: Why is it important to tell the truth? Is it easy or hard? How do you feel when you don't tell the truth? How do others feel? Why do people sometimes not tell the truth? What can happen if we don't tell the truth? What can happen if we do tell the truth? Allow students an opportunity to share situations and examples from their lives. Emphasize to students that although telling the truth will sometimes get them in trouble, lying will always get them in far greater trouble. Help students understand the connection between telling the truth and having others trust them. Tell students you'd like to share a book with them about a little boy who received a great reward and earned the trust of a very important person because he was honest.

Follow-up Questions (after reading)

1. What proclamation did the Emperor issue to the children of the land?

2. Did Ping take good care of his seed? How did he feel when it wouldn't grow?

3. What does Ping think of his friend's suggestion to take another flower to the emperor? What do you think he should have done?

4. What advice did Ping's father give him? How do you think Ping felt when he arrived at the palace and he was the only one with an empty pot?

5. How did the Emperor react to all the flowering pots? How did he react to Ping's pot?

6. Why did the Emperor choose Ping to be the new Emperor? How do you think the Emperor felt toward all the other children? How do you think the children felt?

7. Who do you think learned a lesson in this story? What was the lesson?

Extension Activities

1. Arrange students in small groups and give each student a strip of paper. Ask students to write on their strip a time that they were honest when it was hard to be. Give each group a pile of dirt or potting soil and give each student within the group several seeds and a small paper or plastic cup to plant the seeds in. After students have planted their seeds, have them tape their honesty strip around the outside of the cup. Allow time for students to share their honesty cups with the class – encourage students to clap for each other after they have shared – because being honest is something to cheer about!

2. *Select one student ahead of time to help you with this activity. Before gathering the group, take the student aside ahead of time and instruct him to respond to all of your questions with lies. Have the student sit down in a chair facing the class. Next, ask the student a simple question, such as "Why don't you have your homework today?" As he answers with a lie, (such as "The cat ate my homework"), wrap a strand of yarn around him once. Then ask a follow-up question based on his reply, ("How did the cat get your homework?") As he makes up another answer, wind the yarn around him again. Continue to ask follow-up questions until the student is tangled up in yarn. After you have run out of questions, explain to the class that you asked this person ahead of time to lie to your questions. Discuss the following with the class: a) Ask them if they can see what telling lies can do to someone. Emphasize how one lie almost always leads to another lie, and stress how quickly we can become tangled up and trapped by lies. b) Ask students what some of the benefits are to always telling the truth – help them see that if they tell the truth they won't have to worry about remembering what their last lie was or how to cover it up. c) If you have time, ask several students to share a time they were caught in a lie and had to lie again to cover it up.

Activity with Reproducible

Tell students you're going to give them a chance to practice their "honesty skills," by role playing different scenarios, but first you'd like to role play a situation for them as an example. Ask for a student volunteer to come forward, review the first scenario with them privately, and then have them role play it with you. Once students have seen an example of a role play, ask for volunteers to come up one at a time and draw an honesty scenario from the basket. Depending on the age level and maturity of your students, let the student play the student part, and you play the other role, if applicable (note: the second scenario requires two students). Tell students you'd like them to act out the most honest response they can think of.

Role Play Scenarios for Students

- -

The cashier only charges you for two candy bars when you really bought three.

- -

While on the playground during recess, you see one student take a dollar bill that has accidentally fallen out of another student's pocket without her knowing.

- -

You find a $5 bill in the hallway at school.

- -

A friend asks if he can copy your answers during a science test.

- -

You promised your mom or dad you'd finish your homework while they were out, but you watched TV instead.

- -

You borrowed your friend's video game and lost it.

- -

At the store, you see one of your friends put a bracelet in her pocket without paying for it.

- -

The sign at the mall candy store says, "please don't sample from bins," but you really want a piece and don't have any money with you.

- -

The sign for the amusement park ride says that you must be 12 years old to ride. You are only 10.

- -

The Show-and-Tell Lion

Book: *The Show-and-Tell Lion* by Barbara Abercrombie

Publisher: Margaret K. McElderry

Grade Levels: K-2

Setting: Individual, Small Group, Classroom

Book Description

Matthew has nothing to share for show-and tell – so he decides to tell his class that he has a pet lion at home. His class is fascinated, and Matthew quickly gets in over his head as he creates taller and taller tales about his "pet," causing his classmates to beg for a field trip to Matthews's house to visit the lion. When he confesses the situation to his mom, she tells him he needs to be honest, so Matthew tells the class his lion is in a story he's been writing. This heartfelt story is great for helping children understand the value of honesty and the importance of facing up to bad decisions.

Materials Needed

- ***Extension Activity #1*** - *any blue candy that will stain the lips and tongue*
- ***Extension Activity #3*** - *a copy of Pinocchio by Carlo Collodi*
- ***Activity with Reproducible*** - *crayons/markers, pencils*

Preparation: None needed

Introduction

Have students join you in the reading area and ask them to raise their hands if they know the story of *The Boy Who Cried Wolf*. If students are familiar with the story, allow them time to explain to others what the story is about (if they're not familiar with the story, share it with them.) Ask students how many of them have ever been lied to, and give them a chance to discuss how they felt when it happened. Emphasize that when people lie, it's hard to trust them again – just like in *The Boy Who Cried Wolf*. Discuss with students that people lie for many different reasons, but some common reasons are: to get attention, to not get in trouble, to get something they want, or to not hurt someone's feelings. Explain to students that sometimes a lie starts out small but grows so big that it becomes hard to stop – and tell them that today you'd like to share a book with them about a little boy who finds himself in that same situation.

Follow-up Questions (after reading)

1. Why did Matthew tell his class he had a pet lion? How did his class react?

2. What were some of the things Matthew told his class about Larry?

3. Why do you think it was so hard for Matthew to tell his class the truth? What happened that made him decide to tell the truth? Has it ever been hard for you to tell the truth?

4. How did Matthew feel when he thought about telling his class that he'd made Larry up?

5. What solution did Matthew come up with to explain Larry?

6. How did his class react? How do you think you would have reacted if someone in your class had done what Matthew did? Do you think his classmates will believe Matthew easily from now on?

Extension Activities

1. Give all students one piece of blue candy and ask them to eat it (also eat a piece yourself). After everyone has had a chance to finish their candy, ask students to open their mouths and show you their tongues, gums and lips. Have students look around the room at each other to see that everyone's mouths and tongues are stained blue. Tell students that the effects of telling a lie are very similar – lying will leave a lasting mark on them just like the blue candy did. The candy will leave their mouths blue for a long time, and it will take a while for their mouths to go back to normal. Help students make the connection that when they lie, it will also take a while for things to go back to normal – they will be able to see the results of telling lies for a long time after they've told them. Other people will stop trusting them, they will lose certain privileges and nobody will want to be friends with them.

2. Tell students that we can often tell whether people are telling the truth or not by looking for certain clues in their facial expressions or bodies. Give students several examples of this – such as looking down at the floor, stuttering, seeming nervous, wringing hands, looking away while talking, twisting your mouth, fidgeting, changing the tone of your voice, etc. Tell students you'd like them to think of one thing that's true about themselves, and one thing that's a lie. Then ask for volunteers to come to the front of the class and share both things about themselves – and let the rest of the class guess which thing is a truth and which is a lie.

3. As a follow-up story, read students a copy of *Pinocchio* by Carlo Collodi (the version published by Usborne Books is a good length). Most children will be familiar with this classic story, but it will serve as a great reminder of the often dramatic consequences of lying.

Activity with Reproducible

Discuss with students how quickly and easily a little lie can grow into a big one – like it did for Matthew. Ask students to share examples of times they have told a "little lie" that turned into a "big lie" – and a big deal. You may need to share an example from your own life. Distribute the following activity sheet to students and ask them to draw a picture – with words – of a time when their little lie grew larger.

My Lie Grew and Grew...

Directions: *Think of a time when you told a "little lie" that quickly grew into a "big lie." Draw a picture of what happened, and use words to explain your picture.*

Respect and Manners

Respect for self, respect for others, and respect for things. Virtually every elementary school across the country has some variation of this motto. While respect and manners were once values taught at home, and simply reiterated at school, as our society has changed, so has the expectation that respect and manners will be taught in the schools. One of the first introductions many children have to respect is learning about "The Golden Rule." Learning to treat others as they want to be treated is a concept that's easy to understand, but often more difficult for students to master. Learning to display good manners can be equally difficult for children. As with most things, children will learn and show respect and manners if it's modeled for them appropriately. A key challenge to teaching respect and manners at the elementary level is helping children understand that we don't have to like someone in order to respect them or to show appropriate manners toward them. The books in this section address the importance of showing respect to those who are very different from us, showing respect even when we're angry with someone, and demonstrating good manners toward everyone.

Lilly's Purple Plastic Purse

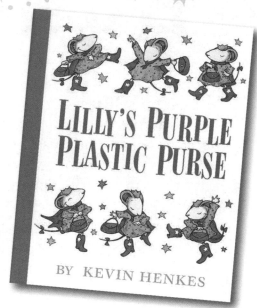

Book: *Lilly's Purple Plastic Purse* by Kevin Henkes

Publisher: Greenwillow Books

Grade Levels: K-2

Setting: Individual, Small Group, Classroom

Book Description

Lilly the mouse loves school, and she especially loves her teacher, Mr. Slinger – until he takes away her musical purse and movie star glasses because she can't stop playing with them in class. Lilly, angry and embarrassed, decides to get revenge with a cruel drawing of her teacher – but after she finds the kind note he left in her purse, she feels horrible and realizes she has to find a way to make things right with Mr. Slinger again.

Materials Needed

- **Introduction -** *recording of "Respect" by Aretha Franklin*
- **Extension Activity #1 -** *(**to be done as book is being read) paper plates, crayons*
- **Extension Activity #2 -** *paper and crayons/markers*

Preparation

- **Extension Activity #1 -** *Give each student a paper plate and have them draw a happy face on one side of the plate, and an angry face on the other side.*
- **Reproducible Activity -** *Copy the scenarios and cut them into strips ahead of time.*

Introduction

Play the song "*Respect*" by Aretha Franklin. As the song is playing, gather students together in a group. Ask if any of them have ever heard the song before. Depending on the age and abilities of the students, you might have to slow the tape down and let them hear each letter, as you write the word on the board. Ask students what respect means to them. Explain to students that respect is honoring others by treating them in a polite way – playing fair, listening to others, using kind words and asking before you borrow things are all great examples. Ask students to share how they feel when someone treats them politely and kindly. Discuss with students that we show people they have value by treating them just like we want to be treated – in a nice way. Help students make the connection between how good they feel when others treat them with respect, and how they can make others feel the same way by treating them with respect in return. Explain to students that this is often called "The Golden Rule." If time permits, discuss some of the following questions with students: How, when and why do we show respect? Who do we show respect to? When is it especially hard to show respect to others? Ask students for examples of times other people have showed respect to them, and for times they have showed respect to others. Tell students you will be sharing a book with them about a girl who's having a hard time showing respect for her teachers and classmates on one particular day.

Follow-up Questions (after reading)

1. What did Lilly do that got her in trouble with Mr. Slinger?

2. Did Lilly show respect or disrespect to her classmates when she was in the circle?

3. How did Lilly feel when Mr. Slinger took her things away? Did Mr. Slinger treat Lilly with respect?

4. What did Lilly do when she went to the Lightbulb Lab? Was she being respectful?

5. How did Lilly feel when she read the note from Mr. Slinger on the way home? Why?

6. What was different about Lilly's next day at school?

7. What did Lilly do to try to apologize to Mr. Slinger?

8. Do you think Lilly learned a lesson? What lesson did she learn?

Extension Activities

1. **Ask students which side of their plate shows how they would feel if someone treated them with respect, and which side of their plate shows how they would feel if someone was disrespectful to them. Tell students that as you are reading the story, you would like them to hold up their "respect side" every time someone in the book shows respect for a person, place or thing, and you'd like them to hold up their "disrespect side" every time someone in the book shows disrespect.

2. Explain to students that, in the book, we learned how important it is to have respect for others, but it's also important to show respect for ourselves and for things. Tell students you'd like them to think about what respect looks like. Give each child a piece of white paper and ask them to divide it into three columns, labeled "respect for self," "respect for others," and "respect for things." Ask students to close their eyes for a moment and get a "picture" in their head of what respect would look like in each situation, and ask them to draw a picture of it. After all students have finished their drawings, have them come to the reading area to share with the rest of the class. Some teachers might want to keep the respect drawings to display around the classroom as reminders.

Activity with Reproducible

Role play for students a respectful way to handle the following situations:

1. You see your teacher walking down the hall with her hands full of books, markers, papers and a lunch bag.

2. One of your classmates is giving a presentation about George Washington, and it's so boring you can hardly stand it.

Tell students you'd like them to have an opportunity to "practice" respect. Ask for pairs of student volunteers to come draw a scenario – one at a time –from the container, read it aloud and demonstrate a respectful way to handle the situation.

Respect Scenarios

You're trying to do your homework, but your older brother has the TV turned up really loud and you can't concentrate.

You want to borrow a friend's favorite toy.

Your mom is talking on the phone and you want to ask her a question.

Your teacher writes your name on the board because you were talking to a friend instead of listening to the teacher's directions.

The man in front of you in line at the grocery store accidentally drops his keys.

Instead of choosing you, your friend chooses another person in your class to pair up with for a project.

You're trying to listen to your teacher, but the other kids at your table are talking to each other loudly and you're having trouble concentrating.

Your mom tells you it's time to get ready for bed, but you want to keep playing.

You open your birthday present from your grandmother and it's a pair of plain white socks.

It's library day and you and another student in your class both want to check out the same book, but there is only one copy.

Piggy Monday

Book: *Piggy Monday: A Tale About Manners* by Suzanne Bloom

Publisher: Albert Whitman & Company

Grade Levels: K-2

Setting: Individual, Group, Classroom

Book Description

The children in Mrs. Hubbub's class are having a big problem with their manners. After many reminders, she warns them that if they do not stop their disrespectful behavior, they will all turn into "swine." Unfortunately, they choose to continue their bad practices and, much to their dismay, they start to grow pig snouts, ears and hooves. The principal, realizing the severity of the situation, calls the manners expert, The Pig Lady. The Pig Lady teaches the students that being respectful is easy and feels good in return. The book is written in rhyming fashion and includes concrete examples of good manners. A matching pig puppet is sold separately.

Materials Needed

- *Introduction - pig puppet (or a large picture of a pig)*
- *Extension Activity #1 - large chart paper or poster board, classroom board games*
- *Extension Activity #2 - 10 sheets of chart paper or poster board, crayons/markers*

Preparation

- *Extension Activity #3 - Invite the school nurse to come speak to the students about good manners as it relates to good hygiene.*

Introduction

Ask students to come to the reading area. Using the pig puppet as a prop, ask students to brainstorm a list of things they know about pigs. If they need help, ask them if pigs are known to be clean or dirty animals. Explain that they are going to hear a story about a classroom of students that turned into pigs. Also, explain that the book uses a different name for the word *pig*, and that word is *swine*.

Follow-up Questions (after reading)

1. What are some of the bad manners that the children were using in the classroom?

2. How do you think the teacher felt as she watched the students be disrespectful to each other?

3. What are some of the consequences of having bad manners? How does it make other people feel when we are disrespectful to them?

4. Which manners are important for our classroom? Do you think it is important for adults to have good manners, too?

5. Do you think the students will remember to have good manners? Explain.

Extension Activities

1. Because game playing is such a beloved activity for children in this developmental stage, hold a "Game-a-thon." Explain to students that they will be divided into small groups to play various classroom board games, such as Candyland, Scrabble Junior, or Sequence for Kids. Before they break up into groups, ask students to brainstorm a list of good manners for game times. Title this list "Game Time Goodies." Write the list on large chart paper, so that it can be displayed during the Game-a-thon. Examples could include the following: Wait for your turn patiently, congratulate a player who does something well or picks a good card, follow the rules and stay cheerful even if you lose the game. Roam around the room as the children are playing and compliment students as you hear and see them exhibit good manners.

2. Building on discussion question #4, explain to students that they are going to create a list of ten important classroom manners. Using 10 sheets of chart paper or poster board, write one manner on each sheet. Divide students into pairs and ask each pair to illustrate one of the manners. Hang the pieces of chart paper around the room so they are visible reminders to the students. Every time a student puts one of these good manners into action, (ongoing) drop a cotton ball into a glass bowl. When the class reaches a certain number, hold a "Good Manners Movie and Munchies Party," where students are allowed to watch a short movie and enjoy snack food munchies.

3. Focus on the idea that good manners help to keep us safe, by inviting the school nurse into the classroom to talk about good hygiene and not spreading germs. Ask her to show students the correct way to sneeze (into the crevice of their arm instead of into their hands) so that they don't pass their germs onto their friends. A great lesson during the cold and flu season!

4. Introduce a new "Manner of the Week" every Monday morning. Write the manner on the board and talk about why it is important. Compliment students as you see them demonstrating each particular manner throughout the week.

Activity with Reproducible

Hand-out the activity sheet and allow students to work in pairs to solve the puzzle.

Answers:

1. names
2. food
3. please, you
4. games
5. sorry
6. toys
7. bossy
8. door

Piggy Monday Manners Puzzle

Directions: *Fill in the missing letters to complete the good manners sentences.*

1. Do not call your friends mean __ __ m __ __.

2. Chew your f __ __ __ with your mouth closed.

3. Say p __ __ __ __ e and thank __ __ __ when you ask for a treat.

4. Take turns when you are playing a g __ __ __.

5. Say "I am s __ __ __ y" if you hurt someone's feelings.

6. Help to clean up the __ __ y __ when you are finished playing with them.

7. Do not be b __ __ __ __. Let everyone make decisions.

8. Hold the d __ __ r for the person behind you.

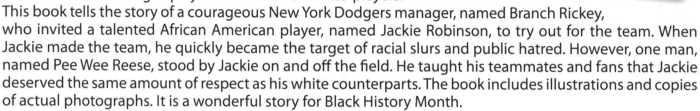

Teammates

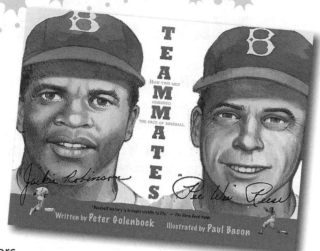

Book: *Teammates* by Peter Golenbock

Publisher: Sandpiper

Grade Levels: 3-5

Setting: Individual, Group, Classroom

Book Description

This non-fiction picture book takes readers back to the 1940's, a time when segregation dominated America, even on the baseball field. Two separate Major Leagues existed – one for Negro players and one for white players. This book tells the story of a courageous New York Dodgers manager, named Branch Rickey, who invited a talented African American player, named Jackie Robinson, to try out for the team. When Jackie made the team, he quickly became the target of racial slurs and public hatred. However, one man, named Pee Wee Reese, stood by Jackie on and off the field. He taught his teammates and fans that Jackie deserved the same amount of respect as his white counterparts. The book includes illustrations and copies of actual photographs. It is a wonderful story for Black History Month.

Materials Needed

- ***Extension Activity #1 -*** *articles on Jackie Robinson, Pee Wee Reese and the Negro Baseball League (only if students do not have access to the internet), 5x7 index cards (one for each group)*

Preparation

- ***Extension Activity #1 -*** *Print articles on Jackie Robinson, Pee Wee Reese and the Negro baseball league if students do not have access to the internet.*

Introduction

Ask students to raise their hand if they enjoy watching or playing baseball. Invite students to share their favorite professional team with the class. Explain to students that a long time ago, in the 1940's, there was one baseball league for white players and another for African American players. They are going to hear a true story about a unique friendship between an African American player and white player. Both men were brave and exhibited mutual respect for one another.

Follow-up Questions (after reading)

1. Describe what life was like for an African American student in the 1940's?

2. How would you describe the Dodgers' manager, Branch Rickey?

3. How do you think Jackie Robinson felt when he made the Dodgers' team?

4. Describe the relationship between Jackie Robinson and Pee Wee Reese?

5. Who were the characters that showed respect toward other people?

6. Put yourself in Pee Wee's shoes. How do you think he was feeling as he walked out to first base during the game? Have you ever been in a situation when you felt this way?

Extension Activities

1. Divide the students into three groups. Invite one group to research the Negro baseball league, one to research Jackie Robinson and the other to research Pee Wee Reese. Ask each group to find 3-5 new facts about their respective subjects. Give each group a 5x7 index card to write their facts. If students do not have access to the internet or a library, print out articles for them in advance and distribute to each group.

2. The book does not tell us about the crowd's response to Pee Wee putting his arm around Jackie in the middle of the baseball game. Lead a short discussion about several different scenarios that could have resulted from Pee Wee's actions.

3. Although the Civil Rights movement occurred during a time of violence, hatred and disrespect, there were also many acts of courage and respect. Ask students if they are aware of other famous individuals that were courageous and showed respect to African Americans during the time of segregation.

Activity with Reproducible

Hand out the activity sheet and allow students to work in pairs to solve the scrambled sentences.

Answers:

1. Pee Wee Reese showed respect to Jackie Robinson.
2. Jackie Robinson was courageous.
3. We all deserve respect.
4. Branch Rickey was a good manager.
5. Pee Wee and Jackie were heros.

Teammates Scramble

Directions: *Unscramble the letters in each of the words to complete the sentences below.*

EEP EWE EREES DSOHWE TCEPSER OT CKAJEI NSROIBNO.

_____ _____ _____ _____ _____ _____

____ _____ _____.

KIECAJ NOSROBNI SAW SOEUCORUGA.

_____ _____ _____

_____.

EW LAL ESRVDEE PETCERS.

____ _____ _____ _____.

CHBRNA PCKRIE SAW A OODG GREMNAA.

_____ _____ _____ __ _____

_____.

EPE EEW NDA CKIEJA EWRE OEHRS.

_____ _____ _____ _____ _____

_____.

The Golden Rule

Book: *The Golden Rule* by Ilene Cooper

Publisher: Abrams Books for Young Readers

Grade Levels: 3-5

Setting: Individual, Group, Classroom

Book Description

When a young boy and his grandfather pass by a billboard that reads, "Do unto others as you would have them do unto you," the boy is intrigued about its meaning. As the grandfather explains the importance of the Golden Rule and its universality, the little boy realizes that it is not always easy to practice. The grandfather agrees and asks him to use his imagination to think about what the world would be like if everyone followed the Golden Rule. Translations of the Golden Rule in Christianity, Judaism, Islam, Hinduism, Buddhism and Native American tribes are included, along with beautiful, large illustrations.

Materials Needed

- *Introduction - bag of Hershey Kisses™ (in gold wrappers)*
- *Extension Activity #1 - drawing paper, crayons and/or markers*
- *Extension Activity #2 - slips of construction paper, stapler*
- *Activity with Reproducible - scenario strips*

Preparation

- *Activity with Reproducible - Cut apart the reproducible into strips.*

Introduction

Ask children to gather at the reading area. Pull a bag of Hershey Kisses™ (wrapped in gold foils) out of a paper bag. Take several Kisses out of the bag and ask students to describe the candy wrapping. When they identify that the candies are wrapped in gold (or golden) paper, ask them what they know about gold. Prompt them to talk about the fact that gold is a very special and valuable metal. Ask them if they have ever heard of something called the Golden Rule, a very special and valuable rule. Explain that you will be reading a book about this important rule. **Children will most likely be excited about the chocolate and eager to learn if they will be able to eat them! Tell students that each will be able to have a Hershey Kiss™ at the end of the lesson.

Follow-up Questions (after reading)

1. Do you think that the grandfather did a good job of explaining The Golden Rule to his grandson? Can you explain what the Golden Rule means in your own words?

2. Have you ever heard of The Golden Rule before? Where did you hear it – home, church, school, etc.?

3. The grandfather explained that The Golden Rule applies to grown-ups and children. Do you know any other rules that apply to grown-ups and children?

4. Has anyone ever heard of the word "empathy?" Do you know what it means? Would you say that The Golden Rule is similar to having empathy for one another?

Extension Activities

1. In the book, the young boy imagines what the world would look like if everyone followed the Golden Rule. Give each student a large piece of drawing paper and ask them to draw a picture of what they think the world would look like if everyone followed the Golden Rule. Allow them to refer back to the book if they need inspiration. **Optional – Use the students' drawings to create a classroom or hallway bulletin board. Title the board "A Golden Rule World."

2. On the last page of the book, the grandfather reiterates the fact that the boy cannot force other people to follow the Golden Rule. Instead, the grandfather says, "You. It starts with you." Give each student a strip of construction paper. Ask them to write down one way they can follow the Golden Rule. Next, ask students to form a large circle. Invite each student to read their idea and then staple their strip to the person's strip beside them, forming a chain. When all of the strips have been connected in a long chain, display the chain in a prominent spot to remind students to follow the Golden Rule.

Activity with Reproducible

In the book, the grandfather asked his grandson to imagine himself in certain situations so that he could practice The Golden Rule. This activity gives students an opportunity to practice "putting themselves in each other's shoes" through live role-plays. First, make a copy of the reproducible and cut the scenarios into strips. Next, divide students into pairs. Give each pair one of the scenario strips (there are two blank strips that can be used to write situations appropriate to the individual class). Tell them to read the scenario together and develop three different ways that they could demonstrate the Golden Rule to the person/people in the situation. Bring the group together and ask each pair to role-play their three ideas to the group.

The Golden Rule Scenarios

Directions for Teacher: *Cut apart the scenario strips and hand one strip to each pair of students.*

- -

A classmate gets picked last when picking teams for the basketball game.

- -

A classmate trips and falls in front of the entire class.

- -

A classmate is teased because her father is in prison.

- -

A new student enters the class and doesn't speak any English.

- -

Your friend finds out that he didn't make the school play.

- -

Your brother/sister's pet hamster dies.

- -

Your teacher is losing her voice and isn't feeling well.

- -

Your parents are rushing around the house, preparing to host your family get-together.

- -

Your classmate has just been diagnosed with a serious illness.

- -

Your friend is being teased because he is the shortest person in the class.

- -

Your elderly neighbor is outside raking her leaves.

- -

_____

- -

_____

- -

Rumors

Although rumors seem harmless to many children, they have the power to literally destroy a child's sense of self-esteem and self-worth. Children can be harassed and humiliated at the hands of a seemingly innocuous rumor. Many children don't understand the deep impact of rumors until they become the victim of a rumor themselves. They simply "repeat" a phrase, word or story told to them without understanding that there are very painful consequences for the person targeted in the rumor. For girls, especially, rumors can be absolutely devastating. While boys typically use physical aggression to handle their anger, hurt or frustration with others, girls use verbal aggression, and this comes most often in the form of vicious rumors. The books in this section help children understand how a simple twist of the truth can turn ugly, the widespread impact rumors can have, and how words can ruin a friendship.

Armadillo Tattletale

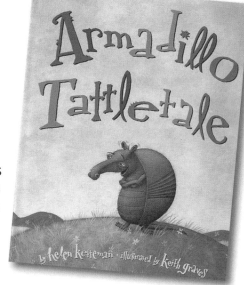

Book: *Armadillo Tattletale* by Helen Ketteman

Publisher: Scholastic Press

Grade Levels: K-3

Setting: Individual, Group, Classroom

Book Description

In the beginning of this fable-like story, Armadillo discovers that his larger-than-average ears are perfect for listening in on other people's conversations. He then decides to create a "ruckus," by twisting the words he hears and spreading rumors among his animal friends. Although his friends try to teach him a lesson by scolding him, he doesn't truly learn his lesson until he runs into a powerful alligator who uses his teeth to clip Armadillo's ears. Armadillo discovers the importance of not telling tales and lives happily ever after with his teeny, tiny ears. Note: this book can also be used to address honesty.

Materials Needed

- *Introduction - armadillo puppet (or picture)*
- *Extension Activity #1 - four colored sheets of paper and a marker*
- *Activity with Reproducible - sentence strips, student scissors, stapler, copies of activity sheet on cardstock paper*

Preparation:

- *Extension Activity #1 - Write each word of the following sentence -* **Recess is canceled today** *- on a different sheet of colored paper and hide the four pieces of paper in various spots around the classroom ahead of time.*

Introduction

Ask students to come to the reading area. Bring out the armadillo puppet (or picture) and ask students if they know the name of this animal. Explain that it is an armadillo, an animal that lives mostly in Latin America. Tell students that they are going to hear a story about an armadillo who liked to spread rumors. Ask them if they have ever heard of a rumor, and ask students to define rumor in their own words. Tell students you'd like to share a book with them about an armadillo who learns some important lessons about honesty, minding his own business and not spreading rumors.

Follow-up Questions (after reading)

1. What did Armadillo like about his big ears? What did he dislike?

2. Why did the different animals tell Armadillo that their words were not for his ears? What did they mean by this?

3. Would you say that Armadillo was dishonest? Why do you think he kept telling lies even after all of the animals got mad at him?

4. Do you think Armadillo enjoyed his new, smaller ears? What were some of the advantages of his new ears?

Extension Activities

1. Explain that there is a "rumor on the loose" and the students need to go on a Rumor Scavenger Hunt to "catch the rumor" before it gets out of the classroom. Their challenge is to find four colored pieces of paper around the classroom. When they find all four pieces of paper, they should bring them back to the reading area and rearrange them to make a sentence. The sentence should read, "Recess is canceled today!" After students arrange the sentence, expect some confusion and anger. Quickly explain to the students that the sentence was just a rumor, but you wanted to show them that confusion, sadness and anger can result from short, but powerful rumors.

2. Play a game of Telephone or Pass it Down the Lane to demonstrate how the truth can become "twisted" as it is passed from person to person. Start the game by whispering a short sentence into one student's ear. Ask them to repeat what they heard to the next person in the circle. The sentence should go around the circle until it reaches the last student. Ask that student to repeat what they heard. Ask the students to explain how the sentence changed from the first person to the last person. Do they believe that this can happen in real life? Talk about what they should do if they hear something and are not sure if it is true.

Activity with Reproducible

Copy the armadillo ears onto heavy cardstock paper. Give a pair of ears to each student and read the "no rumor" words with the students. Ask students to cut out the armadillo ears. After they have cut them out, staple the ears onto a sentence strip and wrap it loosely around their head. Cut off the extra ends and allow the students to wear their armadillo ears for the remainder of the school day.

Armadillo's New Ears

Directions: Read the "no rumors" words on the armadillo's new ears. Cut out the ears carefully.

Telling - **YES!**

Tattling & Rumors - **NO!**

Hen Hears Gossip

Book: *Hen Hears Gossip* by Megan McDonald

Publisher: Greenwillow Books

Grade Levels: K-2

Setting: Individual, Group, Classroom

Book Description

When the hen overhears the cow whisper news to the pig, the hen can't wait to spread the gossip to her friend, the duck. The only problem is that hen does not hear the news correctly! The story grows and changes as the chain of information travels from one animal to another. When the gossip eventually gets back to the hen, she decides to retrace its steps to figure out how the message got twisted. In the end, she learns that life is a lot simpler when you simply mind your own business and avoid gossip!

Materials Needed

- ***Activity with Reproducible*** - *copies of reproducible on cardstock paper, scissors, crayons/markers*

Preparation: None

Introduction

Invite students to the reading area. Explain that you have a special message to share with them. Whisper the message into one student's ear and ask her to send the message around the room by whispering it into the ear of the person beside her. The students should continue passing the message until everyone has heard it. The message should be something simple such as "I have a special book to read to you today." Ask the last student to report back what they heard. Hopefully it will be something similar to what you said. Tell them that you are going to send around a second message. This time, send a more difficult message such as "Ten tired toads told Todd that truly tough toads tackle tigers." If the message changed, ask them why they think it changed. Show the book cover and tell students that they are going to hear a humorous story about a hen and a piece of gossip. Ask them if they have ever heard of the word *gossip*. Challenge them to listen to the story to discover the meaning of the word.

Follow-up Questions (after reading)

1. What is gossip? Why do you think the hen loves it so much?

2. How did the gossip get so twisted as it passed from one animal to the next?

3. How did the hen feel when the gossip got back to her? How did she solve the problem?

4. Have you ever heard a piece of gossip? How did it make you feel?

5. What should you do if you hear gossip in your classroom?

Extension Activities

1. One reason the gossip got twisted in the story is that the animals were not being good listeners. Remind students that good listeners listen with their eyes, ears and brain. Invite one volunteer to come stand beside you. Ask them to tell you about two things they did over the weekend. Demonstrate good listening skills as they speak. When they are finished, repeat back what you heard. If they agree that your account is accurate, they should give you a high-five. If your account is not accurate, they should give you a low-five. Put students in pairs and allow them to do the same exercise with each other. Stress to them that good friends practice good listening.

2. Emphasize the idea that, although the hen made a poor choice by starting the gossip, she did make a good choice by retracing the gossip chain to verify the information. Help students understand that if they hear something and are not sure if it is true, they should go back to the source of the information. Also, help them understand that they have the power to break the chain of gossip by asking students to stand side-by-side and link arms. Remove one of the students from the middle of the chain to show them what happens to the chain of information when one person decides not to spread it – it stops! Encourage them to avoid gossip by not spreading information that they do not think is true or information that may be hurtful to someone else.

Activity with Reproducible

Copy the activity sheet onto cardstock paper. Ask students to cut out the bookmark and color it. Read the gossip sentence together and explain that the bookmark serves as their reminder to avoid spreading rumors.

Hen Hears Gossip

Directions: *Color and cut-out the bookmark. Use it when you read as a reminder of the hen and the trouble that was created by her gossip!*

Mr. Peabody's Apples

Book: *Mr. Peabody's Apples* by Madonna

Publisher: Callaway

Grade Levels: 3-5

Setting: Small Group, Classroom

Book Description

When Tommy Tittlebottom sees Mr. Peabody, a beloved teacher and coach, take an apple from the local fruit market without paying for it, he immediately jumps to the conclusion that Mr. Peabody is a thief, and Tommy spreads the rumor throughout the tiny town of Happville. Although a simple explanation puts the rumor to rest, Mr. Peabody teaches Tommy a valuable and dramatic lesson in the end about just how destructive words can be.

Materials Needed

- **Extension Activity #2 -** *glitter*

Preparation: None needed

Introduction

Have students sit in a large circle. Initiate a discussion with students about the definition of rumors. Explain to students that a rumor is a story that has not been proven true. Ask students to raise their hands if they have ever had someone spread a rumor about them. Then have students close their eyes and ask them to raise their hands if they've ever been the ones to spread the rumor. Allow students to share a couple of real life examples. Have a discussion about why people start rumors (www.pbskids.org/itsmylife) has some excellent information about rumors on their website). Ask students how harmful they think gossip and rumors are on a scale of 1 to 10. Make the point that spreading rumors about someone is a form of bullying – verbal bullying.

Follow-up Questions (after reading)

1. What did Tommy see? What did he do immediately afterward? What could he have done instead?

2. When Tommy told, who did he tell? How did the news spread?

3. How do you think Mr. Peabody felt when he heard what Tommy had done? How do you think you would have felt?

4. How do you think Billy felt when he heard the truth? How did Tommy feel?

5. Do you think Tommy learned his lesson? What do you think Tommy will do next time he sees or hears someone act in a way that doesn't seem right?

Extension Activities

1. Have students play "the telephone game" to illustrate how rumors can become greatly exaggerated after being passed on from person to person. Divide students into two or three small groups and whisper a rumor to the first person in each group (any made up sentence will do – the older the students, the longer the sentence should be). Have that person whisper the rumor in the next person's ear, etc. until the rumor has made it all the way around to the last person in the group. Ask the last person to stand up and repeat what he/she heard. The results are certain to be drastically different from the original sentence. The class will get a good laugh out of this, but it will prove just how unreliable rumors can be.

2. Gather students together in a large circle, and pour a little glitter into one student's hand. Ask that student to shake hands with the person standing next to him/her – go around the circle like this until all students have been "touched" by the glitter. Then ask all students to hold up their palms – point out how much glitter they each have stuck to their hands. Explain that the glitter represents a rumor – it spreads easily and quickly, and once we help pass it on, it sticks to others and is hard to get rid of. Also point out to students that by helping pass the rumor on, they've been "infected" and it will be hard for others to trust them again. Explain that the reverse is also true, however – when we use kind words, respect and compliments, it spreads and sticks to others. Encourage students to start substituting compliments and kind words for rumors so they can start an "epidemic of kindness."

Activity with Reproducible

Review the moral of the story with students – that spreading rumors is like opening a pillow with a thousand feathers and trying to collect them all. Then give all students the following activity sheet and ask them to come up with their own illustration/representation for what spreading rumors is like. Encourage them to think about experiences from their own life, and to be creative. Allow time for students to share their drawings when they're finished.

Spreading a Rumor is Like...

Trouble Talk

Book: *Trouble Talk* by Trudy Ludwig

Publisher: Tricycle Press

Grade Levels: 3-5

Setting: Individual, Group, Classroom

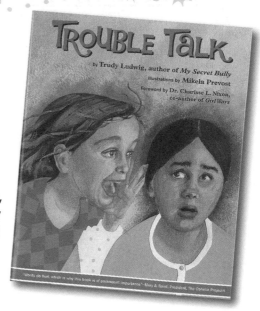

Book Description

When Maya's new friend, Bailey, begins insulting their friends, instigating arguments between classmates and eventually spreading a mean rumor about Maya's parents, Maya is confused about how to handle the situation. Through her conversation with the school counselor, Maya learns the definition of "trouble talk" and how to stand up to someone who is using it to gain power in relationships. The book includes vivid illustrations and a helpful discussion guide.

Materials Needed

- *Introduction - 10 index cards, tape*
- *Extension Activity #2 - poster board or chart paper*

Preparation

- *Introduction - Write ten fictitious rumors on index cards. Tape the index cards under ten of the students' chairs.*

Introduction

Before the students enter the classroom, tape 10 rumors (written on index cards) on the bottom of students' chairs. When students enter the room, ask students to look under their chairs to see if they have one of the ten index cards. If they do, explain that when you say, "go," you will give them three minutes to walk around the classroom and share the information with as many people as they can. When they hear you say, "stop," they should return to their seats. *Note to Counselor: Anticipate a chaotic environment as all of the students scamper around the room trying to spread the information as fast as they can!* After they play the game and are back in their seats, ask different students what they heard around the room. Tell the students who actually had the slips of paper that they are not allowed to respond at this time. Write the different pieces of information on the board. Next, ask the students who had the index cards, if all of the information is correct. Compare the information from the cards with the information on the board. Ask students if it was easy or difficult to remember all of the information "floating" around the room. Lead them through a short discussion about how this activity is similar to rumors and gossip.

Follow-up Questions (after reading)

1. What adjectives would you use to describe Bailey? What adjectives would you use to describe Maya?

2. How do you think Bailey felt when she arrived at school as a new student? Do you think these feelings had any connection with her "trouble talk?"

3. Were you surprised that Bailey spread a rumor about her own friend, Maya? Have you ever had a friend spread a rumor about you? How did you handle it?

4. Do you agree with the school counselor's advice? Have your parents, older siblings, teachers or counselors given you advice on trouble talk that has been helpful? What was their advice?

5. Do you ever hear trouble talk in your classroom? What do you do when you hear it?

6. Is trouble talk only a girl problem or do boys have this problem, too?

Extension Activities

1. Start a discussion about the difference between a rumor and gossip. Inform students that a *rumor is usually a piece of information about an event*. It is unverified and may be true, untrue or a little bit of both. An example of a rumor might be, "Did you hear that anyone who gets in trouble this week will not be able to go on the field trip on Friday?" A rumor is not usually meant to hurt someone's feelings. *Gossip is usually about a person*. It is meant to be hurtful or "juicy" and it causes "drama" as it is spread. It can be true, untrue or a little bit of both. An example of gossip might be, "Did you hear that Julie is having a party and only inviting two girls from the class?" Ask several students to give examples of (fake) rumors or gossip. Have the other students identify their statement as a rumor or a piece of gossip.

2. In small groups, ask students to brainstorm at least five reasons why kids spread gossip or rumors. Next, ask them to come up with at least five strategies for dealing with trouble talk in their classroom. Write these strategies on a piece of poster board. Hang it up in the classroom so that they can quickly locate and utilize the strategies if they hear trouble talk.

Activity with Reproducible

Ask students if they think children are the only ones guilty of trouble talk. Do they believe that adults engage in rumors and gossip, too? Explain to students that you would like them to go home and have a conversation with their parents/guardians about rumors and gossip. Distribute the questionnaire and ask them to go over it with their parents/guardians at home. After students have completed the assignment, ask them to share their conversations with the class.

Trouble Talk Survey

Dear Parent/Guardian: In class today, we read a book about gossip and rumors. Please allow your child to ask you the following questions. Be as honest as you can and use this opportunity to discuss how you have dealt with this difficult subject. Thank you for your support and cooperation!

1. Do adults spread rumors and gossip? _____

   _____

2. Have you ever had a piece of gossip spread about you? How did you handle it? _____

   _____

3. How would you advise me to handle a situation where someone spreads gossip about me?

   _____

4. Why do you think people spread rumors/gossip? _____

   _____

5. Why do you believe gossip is hurtful? _____

   _____

   _____

   Student Signature

   _____

   Parent/Guardian Signature

Self-Esteem

Developing a healthy self-esteem is absolutely crucial for children – the earlier they develop it, the stronger they will be, and the better they will be able to handle change and disappointment later on. We all aspire to have children and students who are happy, confident and well-rounded. Yet how do we instill this confidence in children? How do we build children up who have been torn down by others? How do we help children to feel good about themselves, and to be proud of who they are? Frequent praise and encouragement from teachers and parents plays a huge role, and helping children understand and embrace the things about them that make them unique is crucial. It's also important to teach children to surround themselves with friends who make them feel good about themselves, and who value their differences. The books in this section address self-esteem through a variety of unique characters who are struggling to find their place in the world.

A Bad Case of Stripes

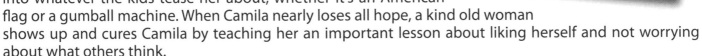

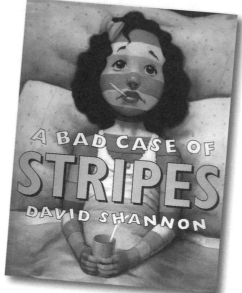

Book: *A Bad Case of Stripes* by David Shannon

Publisher: Scholastic Paperbacks

Grade Levels: 2-5

Setting: Individual, Group, Classroom

Book Description

Young Camila Cream spends all of her time worrying about what other people think of her. She even stops eating her beloved lima beans because she's afraid the other kids will think she's weird. Her fears intensify when she wakes up one morning with multi-colored stripes covering her body. What will the other kids say about her? When she goes to school, Camila discovers that her body changes into whatever the kids tease her about, whether it's an American flag or a gumball machine. When Camila nearly loses all hope, a kind old woman shows up and cures Camila by teaching her an important lesson about liking herself and not worrying about what others think.

Materials Needed

- *Extension Activity #1 - bag of jelly beans, two sandwich bags*
- *Activity with Reproducible - reproducible copied on multi-colored paper*

Preparation

- *Extension Activity #1 - Separate jelly beans into two sandwich bags, one with only yellow jelly beans and the other with multi-colored jelly beans.*

Introduction

Write the words *self-esteem* on the board. Ask students if they have ever seen or heard these words. After gathering student responses, explain that self-esteem means taking pride in yourself or appreciating yourself for who you are. Next, ask students if they think it is important to have self-esteem. Show them the book and explain that they are going to hear a story about a girl named Camila Cream. At the end of the book, they will have to decide if Camila had self-esteem.

Follow-up Questions (after reading)

1. Do you think Camila had self-esteem? Explain your answer.

2. What did Camila do in the beginning of the book that resulted in her "growing stripes?"

3. Why do you think the medical "experts" were unable to diagnose the problem?

4. What lesson did the kind old woman teach Camila?

5. Put yourself in Camila's shoes. Have you ever been scared that you would be teased for doing something different?

Extension Activities

1. Show the students two sandwich bags filled with jelly beans, one filled only with yellow jelly beans and the other filled with multi-colored jelly beans. Ask students to raise their hands and vote for the bag they would choose to eat. If there are any students that choose the all-yellow bag, ask them to explain their choice. Next, ask the students who chose the multi-colored bag to explain their choice. Talk about the fact that the multi-colored bag is more interesting to look at and has more variety than the all-yellow bag. Even if you like yellow jelly beans, you would probably be tired of them about halfway through the bag. Relate this to their classroom and how each of them brings special talents and personality traits to the community, which helps creates a vibrant and colorful learning community.

2. Play a game of Self-Esteem Scramble. Instruct students to stand in a circle. Ask one student to vacate her spot and stand in the center of the circle. Keep the vacated spot empty. Ask all students to think about one of their unique qualities or talents. The student in the center of the circle will state her unique quality and then say, "Scramble!" If there are any other students that have the same talent/quality they have to leave their spot and try to occupy one of the vacant spots. At the same time, the person in the middle is also trying to find an empty spot in the circle. The last person to find a spot goes to the middle of the circle and becomes the next caller.

Activity with Reproducible

Photocopy the reproducible on different colors of paper. Ask students to brainstorm one talent they have that is "different" than most of the kids in the class. If they do not want to use a talent, they can also think about something that sets them apart from other students. For example, maybe they have traveled to an exotic country or play a unique instrument. Maybe they enjoy an unusual vegetable like lima beans. Ask students to complete the self-esteem sentence and draw an illustration to accompany it. When they finish their picture, invite them to bring their paper up to the front of the room. Staple or glue the papers side-by-side on a bulletin board or large piece of bulletin board paper. When everyone is finished, gather the students in front of their multi-colored Self-Esteem Quilt and ask them to share what they wrote. Hang the quilt in the hallway or classroom.

Our Self-Esteem Quilt

I am unique because _____

_____

_____ .

Elmer

Book: *Elmer* by David McKee

Publisher: HarperCollins

Grade Levels: K-2

Setting: Individual, Small Group, Classroom

Book Description

Elmer is the only elephant in the jungle that is a multicolored patchwork instead of being gray. In spite of his cheerful personality, Elmer begins to feel conspicuous and he gets tired of being different. When he discovers some berries that can turn him gray like the other elephants, he thinks his problems are solved. Yet when everyone starts wondering where their old friend is, Elmer realizes the importance of being himself.

Materials Needed

- *Extension Activity #1 - finger paint, heavy white paper*
- *Extension Activity #2 - plain white paper cut into 8 x 8 squares, crayons or markers, two pieces of poster board.*

Preparation

- *Extension Activity #1 - Set up various colored paints in different containers – each group of four should have three or four containers with different paint colors in each.*
- *Extension Activity #2 - Cut plain white paper into enough 8 x 8 squares so every student has one.*

Introduction

Discuss and define the following words with students – differences, diversity and self-esteem. Have students share ways people are different, and ways they are alike. Help them understand there are more ways all of us are alike than different, and that our differences are what make us special and unique. Show students a photograph or magazine picture of a rainy day and a sunny day. Explain to students that we need both kinds of days in the world – the rainy day is gray and cloudy, but rain helps plants grow, and we get to use pretty umbrellas and splash in puddles, etc. Ask students why they like sunny days. OR…show students a large box of crayons and point out how many different colors there are in the box. Ask students why they think there are so many colors – would they rather have a lot of different colors to choose from when coloring/drawing a picture, or one color. Why? Help them understand that colors are like people – we need all types to make a beautiful picture. Tell students you would like to share a story with them about an elephant that is a little bit different from his friends, and is unhappy about it.

Follow-up Questions (after reading)

1. Why wasn't Elmer happy? What made him different from other elephants?

2. What did Elmer do at the berry bush? Why?

3. How do you think Elmer felt when none of the other elephants recognized him?

4. Why do you think the elephants were all so serious? What did Elmer do to make them laugh?

5. What did the elephants decide to do in Elmer's honor each year?

6. Do you think Elmer learned a lesson from his experience? What lesson?

7. Do you have any friends who look different from you? How would you feel if all your friends looked exactly like you?

Extension Activities

1. Divide students into groups of 3-4, and let each group share several small containers of finger paint. Give each student a piece of heavy paper suitable for paint. Ask students to dip their fingers and thumbs in the variety of different colored finger paints to create a multi-colored elephant. Give students an opportunity to share their unique elephants with the class when they are finished. Point out that not only are all of the elephants differently colored, but they are totally unique because each person's fingerprints are different.

2. Give each student a piece of plain white 8 x 8 paper and ask them to draw one thing they like about themselves – whether it's a physical attribute, a talent or a special skill. Have them write words to accompany the drawing. When all students are finished, allow them time to share their drawings with the class. Once all drawings have been shared, you can mount the drawings onto a large piece of poster board – students will then have their own classroom quilt of self-esteem.

Activity with Reproducible

Ask students to raise their hand if they've ever seen a rainbow. Talk with students about when we see rainbows – on days when the sun suddenly comes out after it has rained. Emphasize the fact that rainbows help make everything brighter, beautiful, and more colorful – just like each of them have their own "colors" they contribute to the world to make it a better place. Tell students you'd like them each to make their own rainbows, based on the colors that make up their lives. Distribute the rainbow worksheets and ask students to fill in the color that represents them in each line of the rainbow.

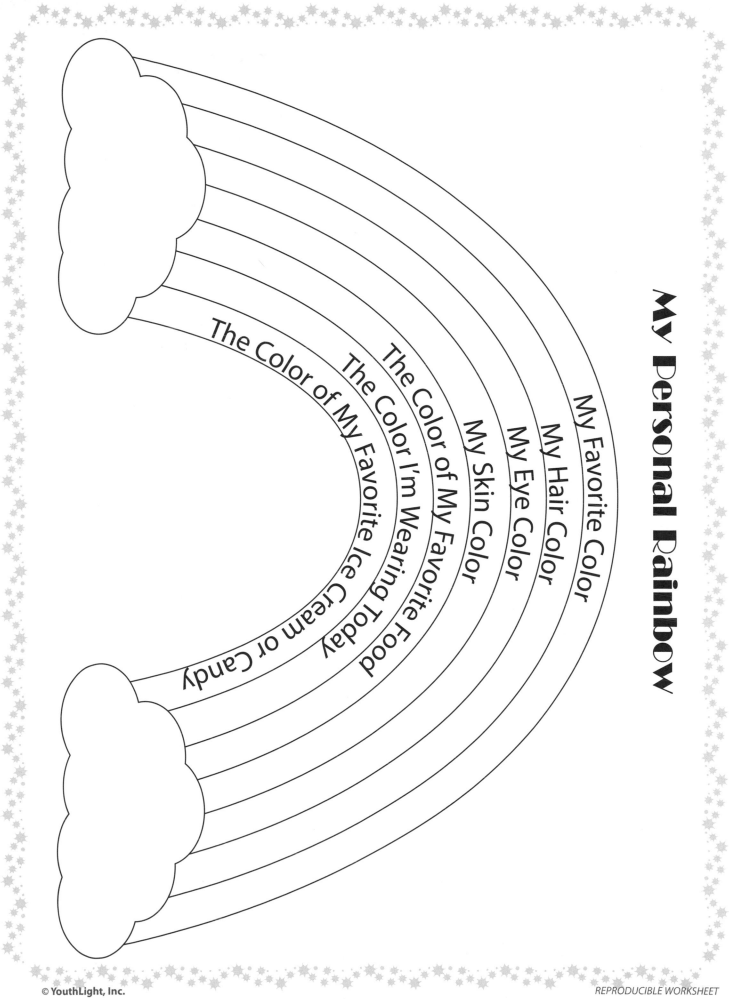

My Personal Rainbow

My Favorite Color

My Hair Color

My Eye Color

My Skin Color

The Color of My Favorite Food

The Color I'm Wearing Today

The Color of My Favorite Ice Cream or Candy

Finklehopper Frog

Book: *Finklehopper Frog* by Irene Livingston

Publisher: Tricycle Press

Grade Levels: K-2

Setting: Individual, Group, Classroom

Book Description

When Finklehopper Frog looks out the window and sees his animal friends jogging, he decides to pick up the sport, too. After shopping for the perfect, wildly-colored jogging suit, he sets off for his first official jog. He soon realizes that his body was made for hopping, not jogging. Despite being teased by the other animals, Finklehopper hops on with determination. Just as Finklehopper is about to give up, he meets Ruby Rabbit, a fellow "hopper." Ruby compliments Finklehopper on his running suit, encourages him to be proud of the way he moves, and reminds him to always be true to himself. He gives all of us the important message that there is "room for everyone" on the running track of life!

Materials Needed

- ***Extension Activity #1 -*** *crayons or markers, chart paper*

Preparation

- ***Extension Activity #2 -*** *Invite someone with a physical disability to come speak with the students about the disability and how to show respect to those with disabilities.*

Introduction

Ask students to come to the reading area. Write the words *self-esteem* on the board. Ask students if they have ever heard of these words. Explain that the words mean "feeling good about yourself." Tell them that they will be hearing a story about a frog who learned the importance of self-esteem and having treasured friends to encourage him along the way.

Follow-up Questions (after reading)

1. What was it that made Finklehopper want to jog in the beginning of the story? Have you ever wanted to do something just because you saw someone else doing it?

2. How do you think Finklehopper felt about his new running suit? What clues did you get from the story?

3. What made the other animals tease Finklehopper? How did Finklehopper Frog react?

4. Have you ever been teased for looking differently or doing something differently? How did you feel? How did you react?

5. What did Ruby do or say to make Finklehopper feel good about himself again?

6. Do you think Finklehopper had good self-esteem? Explain.

Extension Activities

1. To emphasize the power of encouragement, ask students to reflect on the words that Ruby Rabbit used with Finklehopper. Re-read the pages in the book where Ruby encourages Finklehopper. On chart paper, challenge students to think of ten encouraging phrases they could use with their classmates. Hang the paper in the room so they have a constant reminder of positive words they can use with their friends. Provide a few examples if students get stuck in the beginning. Examples include, "Way to go! You look nice today. Don't give up! You can do it!"

2. This is a wonderful book to introduce the topic of physical disabilities. On the last page of the book, the animals are shown running together, including a caterpillar in a wheelchair. Ask the students if they have ever seen someone riding in a wheelchair. Introduce other tools that help people move, such as a cane, walker, leg brace, etc. Talk about ways that we can show kindness and sensitivity to people who use these tools. Consider inviting someone with a physical disability into the classroom to speak to the students.

3. Play animal charades. Using the animals from the book, choose one student to act out an animal without using any words. Encourage them to demonstrate how the animal moves. Allow the other students to guess the animal. Take turns until everyone has had the opportunity to be an actor or actress.

Activity with Reproducible

Distribute the reproducible of Finklehopper in a blank, colorless running suit. Ask them to design a new running suit for Finklehopper, reminding them to use their imagination to create a suit that reflects Finklehopper's independent personality.

Finklehopper Frog's New Jogging Suit

Directions: *Please design a new jogging suit for Finklehopper Frog. Remember that he likes imaginative suits with plenty of color!*

Name _____

Stand Tall, Molly Lou Melon

Book: *Stand Tall, Molly Lou Melon* by Patty Lovell

Publisher: Putnam Juvenile

Grade Levels: 1-3

Setting: Individual, Small Group, Classroom

Book Description

Molly Lou Melon is tiny and clumsy, with buck teeth and a voice that sounds like "a bullfrog being squeezed by a boa constrictor," but she doesn't mind. Her grandmother has always told her to walk proud, smile big and sing out loud, and that's exactly what she does. Yet Molly Lou's self-assurance is tested when she moves to a new town and is relentlessly teased by Ronald Durkin, a cruel bully. However, Molly Lou remembers what her grandmother told her, and she ends up putting Ronald Durkin in his place.

Materials Needed

- *Introduction - white paper, scissors for each student*
- *Extension Activity #2 - one or two strips of white paper for each student*
- *Extension Activity #3 - crown (reproducible), large chair, piece of brightly colored paper, sentence strips*
- *Activity with Reproducible - a rectangular tissue box*

Preparation

- *Extension Activity #3 - Make a sign out of colored paper that says, "Compliment Throne," and copy and cut out the included crown ahead of time. Attach sentence strips to crown.*
- *Activity with Reproducible - Copy and cut out the included compliment box template ahead of time.*

Introduction

Immediately start off the class by giving each student a blank, white sheet of paper and asking them to fold it into smaller and smaller triangles. Then have them take scissors and cut into the triangle at various places along the edges. (They are making a snowflake, and many of them will quickly guess this, but don't give it away yet). Tell them they can be as creative with their design as they want, but they can't cut all the way into the triangle. Do not allow students to "open" their snowflakes – ask them to put their triangles aside when they've finished cutting. Tell students you'd like to share a book about a special girl named Molly Lou Melon.

Follow-up Questions (after reading)

1. How did Molly Lou Melon feel about herself at the beginning of the story?

2. What were some things that were unique about Molly Lou Melon? Have you ever felt different from other people? Do you think being different is good or bad?

3. Who helped Molly Lou Melon believe in herself? What were some of the things Molly Lou Melon's grandmother told her?

4. Is there someone in your life who helps you believe in yourself? What are some things that person says to make you feel good about yourself?

5. Why do you think Ronald Durkin was so mean to Molly Lou Melon? How do you think it made her feel? Do you think you would be able to "stand tall" if someone was teasing you like that?

6. Do you think Ronald Durkin learned a lesson from Molly Lou Melon? Have you ever learned a lesson from someone who was different from you?

Extension Activities

1. Have the students open their triangles at the same time, and then ask them to be as "quiet as snow" as they look around to see what everyone else's snowflakes look like. Ask students to comment on similarities and differences they notice between snowflakes. Go around the room and ask students to share something that makes them unique.

2. As a group, have students think of their own positive affirmations that might boost them up when they're having a tough day. Have students write one positive thought on a strip of paper. When all students are finished, give them all an opportunity to share their positive thoughts and then post the thoughts all around the classroom.

3. Ask students if they know what a compliment is. Help students understand that receiving compliments from others makes us feel good about ourselves and usually boosts our self-confidence – make sure students understand the difference between a sincere compliment and an insincere one. Allow several students to share compliments they have received from others, and ask them how it felt to receive the compliments. Tell students that when you receive a compliment it makes you feel appreciated and important – you feel like "royalty." Tell students you'd like to give each of them a chance to feel like a queen or king. Place an adult-sized chair at the front of the classroom, and hang the Compliment Throne sign over it. Ask which student would like to be "crowned with compliments" first, and ask that child to come up and sit on the Compliment Throne. Place the crown on the student's head and introduce your new "queen" or "king" to the class. Tell the class that you'd like them to take turns crowning their "fearless leader" with compliments – and allow the queen/king to call on students one by one. Allow each student 1-2 minutes in the Compliment Throne. When everyone that wants a turn has had one, go around the room and ask students how they're feeling about themselves and ask them to share the favorite compliment they received.

Activity with Reproducible

Explain that the class is going to have a "compliment box." Place the box in a special spot in the classroom with a stack of paper slips next to it. Every day, if students see kind things happening in the classroom, or if they just want to compliment another student (I like Sara's new haircut, Jose's glasses make him look really smart) they can write a compliment on the slip of paper. They may choose to sign it or not. Encourage students to write compliments about how people treat them and about people's personality characteristics, rather than their appearance. Once a week, the classroom teacher can allow time to read the compliments aloud (or you can choose to wait and read the compliments aloud whenever you have scheduled guidance in that classroom.) Tell students you'd like them to start their compliment box today by writing down one or two compliments each and dropping them in the box (or you can choose to read this first batch aloud).

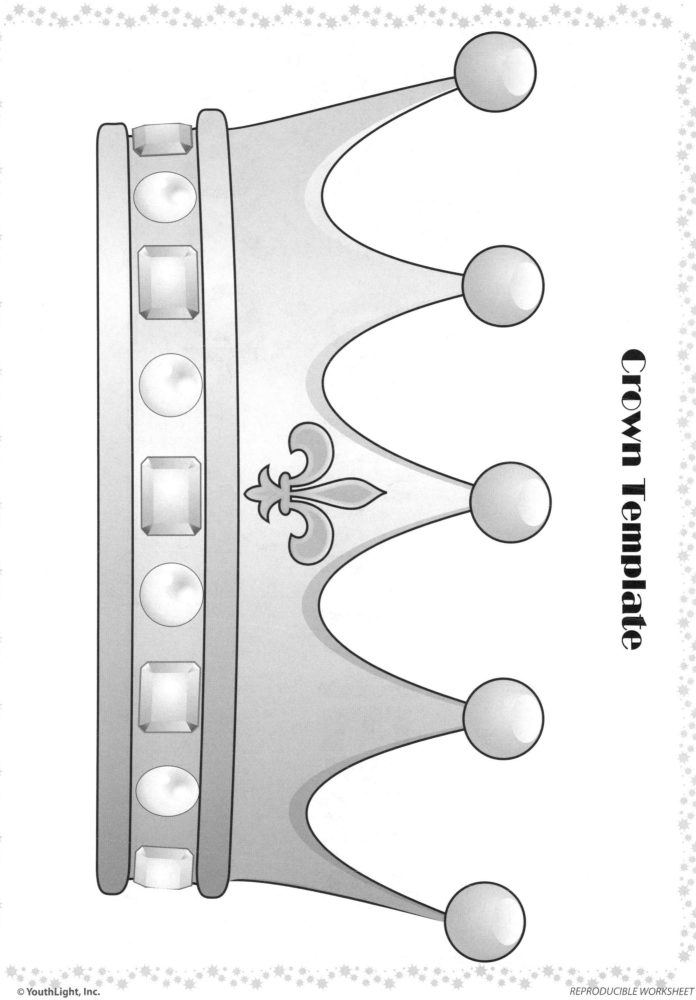

Crown Template

REPRODUCIBLE WORKSHEET

BOX OF COMPLIMENTS

Social Skills

As counselors, teachers or parents, we all have expectations that our children will interact in certain ways, whether they are at home, in school, or in a public place. Good manners, great listening skills, respect for personal space and no tattling rank high on the list of skills we'd like our children to have. These skills are taught in the early elementary grades, and reinforced in every grade thereafter. Children of all ages are under more pressure today than they were decades ago, and with the added pressure comes added stress. This added stress often manifests itself in inappropriate interpersonal behavior. An important indicator of positive social skills is whether children understand the need to respect everyone – even though they may not know them personally, or like them as friends. The books in this section help children understand the importance of respecting their peers, parents and teachers – whether by respecting their personal space, practicing good listening skills or learning why it's not okay to tattle.

A Bad Case of Tattle-Tongue

Book: *A Bad Case of Tattle Tongue* by Julia Cook

Publisher: CTC Publishing

Grade Levels: 1-3

Setting: Individual, Small Group, Classroom

Book Description

Josh tattles on absolutely everyone. He tattles so much that nobody wants to be around him and he loses all his friends. Then one day he wakes up to discover that his tongue has grown incredibly long, turned yellow and is covered with bright purple, itchy spots. Does he learn a lesson from his terrible case of Tattle Tongue? A humorous book that helps students understand the difference between unnecessary tattling and appropriate telling.

Materials Needed

- ***Extension Activity #1 -*** *paper, a container to draw from*
- ***Extension Activity #2 -*** *one sheet of white drawing paper for each student, crayons/markers*
- ***Activity with Reproducible -*** *one red and one yellow crayon for each student*

Preparation

- ***Extension Activity #1 -*** *Write the 8 scenarios down on separate strips of paper, (don't write the answers on the strips) cut them out, and place them in a container to draw from.*

Introduction

Invite students to the reading area and ask them to raise their hands if they've ever had someone tattle on them. Ask the students who raised their hands to share their stories, and ask them how they felt when it happened. Have students tell you why they think people tattle – and help them come to an understanding that we usually tattle on someone because we want to get that person in trouble. Explain to students that there *are* times when it's important to let a teacher or other adult know about something – but only if someone is hurt, sick, crying or in danger. Tell students this is known as reporting, (*note: in the book it's called "warning") and give several examples of things it would be important to report to an adult. Teach students that an easy way to remember the difference between tattling and reporting is that reporting is telling to get someone **out** of trouble, while tattling is telling to get someone **in** trouble. Tell students you'd like to share a story with them about a little boy who ends up with a serious problem because of tattling.

Follow-up Questions (after reading)

1. What kinds of things did Josh tattle about in the beginning of the story?

2. How did the people in Josh's class feel about him? Have you ever stayed away from someone because that person tattled too much?

3. What did Josh's mom tell him would happen if he kept tattling? Did it happen?

4. What did Josh overhear that he chose **not** to tell an adult about? Do you think that was a good choice or a bad choice? What did the Tattle Prince say about this?

5. What did the Tattle Prince say the difference was between tattling and warning/reporting?

6. What were the four Tattle Rules? Can you give an example of what Josh did to break each rule? Which Tattle Rule do you think is the hardest one to follow?

7. What happened when Josh went back to school? Do you think he ever got Tattle Tongue again?

Extension Activities

1. Divide the class into two teams. Give each team 8 pieces of scrap paper. Have teams take turns sending one student to the front of the room to draw a tattling scenario out of the cup. The student who draws a scenario should read the statement aloud to the class. Then allow each team 30 seconds to make a decision on which of the four "Tattling Rules" the scenario fits under. One person on each team should be responsible for writing down the decision of the team (**D**anger Ranger, **P**roblem Solver, **N**ow or Later or **M**.Y.O.B.). When time is up, ask each team to hold up the letter that represents their decision (D, P, N, or M). One point is awarded for every correct answer.

   ** Note to counselor: Write down and cut out these scenarios ahead of time.

   - You see a student in the cafeteria shoving another student against the wall and threatening to beat that student up at the bus stop. (DR)

   - A girl in your class sticks out her foot to trip you every time you get up to sharpen your pencil. (DR)

   - The student who sits next to you in class always tries to copy your answers (PS)

   - The student who sits behind you in math is always chewing gum loudly and it distracts you (PS)

   - A student in your art class always takes your favorite set of paints (NL)

   - Your older brother is hogging the T.V. remote and your mom is on the phone (NL)

   - One of the students at your lunch table brings in a soda for lunch – which is not allowed – and shares it with another student at the table. (M.Y.O.B.)

   - You see two students in your class using markers to do their assignment, and your teacher doesn't allow your class to use markers. (M.Y.O.B.)

2. Divide the class into four groups and assign each group one of the four "Tattling Rules" from the book - Be a Danger Ranger, Be a Problem Solver, Now or Later and M.Y.O.B. Give each student a piece of white paper and tell them you'd like each of them to draw an example of a "tattle" that fits their assigned rule, and write their tattle underneath it. Tell students you'd like them to come up with their own ideas and not use the examples from the book. When all students have finished, have each group come to the front of the class and present all the different examples. Depending on the size of your class, you should have between 4-7 tattling examples per group – this is a great project to post on classroom or hallway walls!

Activity with Reproducible

Tell students you'd like them to use what they learned today about tattling versus reporting by completing the following activity sheet. Distribute the sheet to students and read each of the scenarios on the tongue aloud as students follow along. Tell students if they think the scenario is an example of tattling, they should color the circle yellow, and if they think it's an example of reporting, they should color the circle red. *Note: Depending on students' age and ability level, they can read all the scenarios themselves and work independently.

Tattling or Reporting?

Directions: Read the statements that are listed in each of the circles on the tongue. If you think a statement is an example of tattling, color the circle yellow. If you think a statement is an example of reporting, color the circle red.

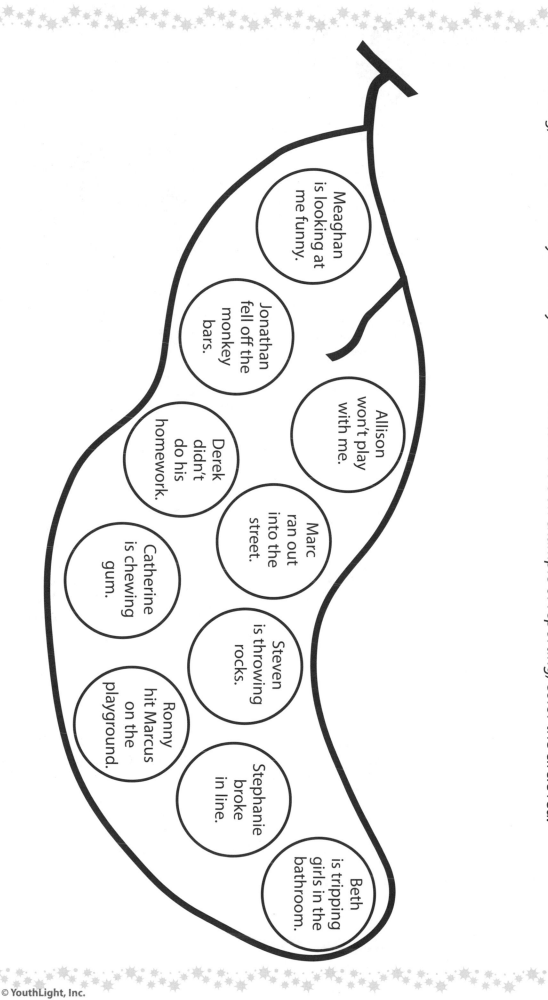

Meaghan is looking at me funny.

Jonathan fell off the monkey bars.

Allison won't play with me.

Derek didn't do his homework.

Marc ran out into the street.

Catherine is chewing gum.

Steven is throwing rocks.

Ronny hit Marcus on the playground.

Stephanie broke in line.

Beth is tripping girls in the bathroom.

Don't Squeal Unless It's a Big Deal:
A Tale of Tattletales

Book: *Don't Squeal Unless It's a Big Deal: A Tale of Tattletales* by Jeanie Franz Ransom

Publisher: Magination Press

Grade Levels: K-2

Setting: Individual, Group, Classroom

Book Description

Mrs. McNeal has nineteen little piglets in her classroom. They are very good students except for one BIG problem – tattling! She finds herself mediating small disagreements all day long, from pigtail pulling to name calling. She seizes a teachable moment to demonstrate the difference between "big deals" and "kid-sized problems." When she falls and hurts herself in the classroom, the students call for help and prove that they know the difference between the two types of problems. A helpful note to parents and teachers is included at the back of the book.

Materials Needed

- ***Activity with Reproducible*** - *pencils*

Preparation: None

Introduction

Invite students to come to the reading area. Show the book's front cover and explain that you are going to read a book about a classroom that has a BIG problem. Ask them to brainstorm about this problem. What could it possibly be? Tell them that it is their job to listen closely to the story to discover the problem and how they solved it in the classroom.

Follow-up Questions (after reading)

1. What was the problem in Mrs. McNeal's classroom?

2. Mrs. McNeal taught the students the difference between "big deals" and "kid-sized problems." What were some of the "kid-sized problems" that were happening in her class? What was the one "big deal problem" that happened in her class?

3. Have you ever heard someone being called a tattletale? What does this mean?

4. How does it feel when someone tattles on you? How would you handle the situation?

5. What rules should our classroom have about tattling?

Extension Activities

1. Building on follow-up question #2, give students several examples of "little deals" and "big deals," reiterating that big deals need to be reported to adults immediately (i.e. issues of safety). "Little deals" should be problem-solved first by students, then by adults if the students were not successful in finding a resolution. Ask students to stand up in the circle. Explain that you are going to give them several examples and they are going to have to decide if they are "big deals" or "little deals." If they are little deals, the students should hold their hands close together. If they are big deals, they should spread their arms out wide to their sides. After you have played several rounds, ask students if they would like to share examples with the class.

2. This book is a natural introduction to using "I Messages" as a problem-solving strategy. Teach students the basic format of "I Messages" and emphasize that these types of messages promote problem solving over placing blame. Using the tattletale situations from the book, allow students to give "I Messages" from each character's point of view. Allow the students to role-play the scene to add extra excitement.

"I Message" Format

"I feel _____ when _____.

Please _____."

Activity with Reproducible

Distribute the activity sheet and ask students to find the hidden words in the word search. Allow students to work in pairs or small groups.

Don't Squeal Unless It's a Big Deal

Directions: *Find the hidden words in the puzzle.*

```
E V L O S M E L B O R P G E L
L A E D G I B Z C Q W N L A U
T D Y Z C Q E L N Y I A E W N
O S C P K J A Y S L T D A R T
K A S U Y S P Q L E E F H Z S
W E W L S O Q A L L K K J M D
P P H R L W C T T O M A W S V
T R O I X E T T R V R B E A H
V O A F M A I Q E F E K Q S G
M P C A T L P V H E P V M O R
D D N Z M R U N C N O I O P X
S D N E I R F T A F E Z M G S
T B B T M A F N E R A U P K E
I D S W W U D N T H R A Q A P
S Q U E A L I K N R L G T A Q
```

WORD BANK

BIG DEAL	TATTLETALE	TEACHER
SQUEAL	CLASSROOM	PROBLEM SOLVE
FRIENDS	NAME CALLING	LITTLE DEAL

Listen Buddy

Book: *Listen Buddy* by Helen Lester

Publisher: Scholastic, Inc.

Grade Levels: K-2

Setting: Individual, Small Group, Classroom

Book Description

Buddy the bunny has enormous ears, but they definitely don't help him listen any better. He manages to misinterpret all of his parents' requests (dragging in a chopped off bed when his mom asks for a slice of bread). When Buddy ventures out on his own for the first time, he selects the wrong route and ends up at the cave of the Scruffy Varmint, where chaos erupts as Buddy tries to help the cranky creature cook soup. When the varmint decides that he'd rather eat stew made from "the Bunny rabbit who never listens," Buddy finally gets the message.

Materials Needed

- ***Introduction*** - *bunny ears (you can usually get these at the Dollar Store)*
- ***Extension Activity #1*** - *a CD of a fun, energetic children's song that has a repetitive song or phrase – I use "The Freeze Song."*
- ***Extension Activity #3*** - *drawing paper*
- ***Extension Activity #4*** - *a tape recording of various sounds*
- ***Activity with Reproducible*** - *a basket or container*

Preparation

- ***Extension Activity #4*** - *Make a tape recording of various sounds. Some examples: A dog barking, water running, a door shutting, a toilet flushing, whistling, clapping, fingers snapping, an alarm clock going off, a cell phone ringing, a microwave beeping, a car horn, knocking on door, a doorbell, a baby crying, etc.*
- ***Activity with Reproducible*** - *You'll need to copy and cut out the bunny ear scenarios ahead of time.*

Introduction

Have students gather around in a circle. As everyone starts to sit down, put your bunny ears on. Innocently ask students if they notice anything different about you. When they immediately point out your ears (usually with lots of giggling) ask students what we use our ears for. When listening is given as an answer, ask students to raise their hand if they can tell you what it means to be a good listener. Have students explain why being able to listen is important – at school, at home and with our friends. Ask students what some consequences might be if they don't listen. Have students raise their hands if they've ever had a hard time listening, and allow several students to share examples of when and why listening was hard for them. Tell students you're going to read them a book about a rabbit that has a hard time listening, and gets into a mess because he doesn't listen carefully.

Follow-up Questions (after reading)

1. What are some things Buddy's parents asked him to do that he had trouble doing? Why did he have trouble?

2. What did Buddy's parents warn him about?

3. How and why did Buddy end up at the cave of the Scruffy Varmint?

4. Did Buddy listen to the Scruffy Varmint at first? What are some silly mistakes he made?

5. What did it take for Buddy to finally listen? Do you think he will have any more problems listening from now on?

Extension Activities

1. Have students gather around in a circle, while standing. Explain to them that you're going to play a fun song, and you'd like them to dance around and be silly, but that every time they hear a particular word (you choose whatever word is most repetitive in the song) you want them to "freeze" - demonstrate what freezing looks like. Tell them it's okay to have fun with it, but in order to play the game correctly and know when to freeze, they need to listen carefully.

2. Explain to students that you are going to do a role play with a student to demonstrate listening skills. Tell students you'd like them to watch carefully to see whether or not you are being a good listener. Ask for a student volunteer (be sure to pick a verbal child who won't have trouble talking a lot). Whisper to the student that you are going to be a bad listener and he/she should just keep talking. You can ask your volunteer to talk about her favorite TV show, family, weekend plans, what she wants to be when she grows up, etc. Role play bad listening (move around in your chair, look around the room while the student is talking, tap your feet on the floor repeatedly, interrupt, whisper to another student, look at watch, play with your pencil) for two to three minutes. Have children explain why it looks like you're not listening. Ask the volunteer how it felt to talk to you when you were being such a bad listener.

3. Ask students which body parts we use to listen. Talk about the five important steps of listening – eyes on speaker, hands to self, body still, mouth closed, ears and brain "on." Draw picture clues on the board to represent each listening step, and explain to students how and why each step is important. Have each student trace his hand and write the five steps of listening on his five fingers. Tell students that for the rest of the year, when you hold your hand up facing them, that's their cue to listen carefully.

4. Tell students you'd like to give them a chance to practice their listening skills by seeing how well they can identify some common sounds. Have students remain in their desks while you play the sound tape. Play one sound at a time, and afterward, stop the tape to ask students what sound they heard.

Activity with Reproducible

Tell students you'd like them to think about whether they are a great listener, a good listener, an okay listener or a bad listener. Then call out each level of listening again – one at a time – and have students raise their hands to indicate their listening skill level. Tell students that one of the main ways they practice listening skills every day is by following directions. Ask for volunteers who would like to test their listening skills by following some simple directions. Have students come to the front one at a time and choose a bunny ear from the basket. Remind all students to listen carefully as you read the directions on the bunny ear. Ask the student volunteer to follow the directions to show that she has listened well – warn students that some directions may be silly ones.

How Well Can You Listen?

Jump up and down three times, clap your hands and say your name.

Go to your desk, get a red crayon and black crayon and bring them to me.

Choose a friend and ask that friend to line up behind you at the door.

Go to the bookshelf, choose three books and put them on your desk.

Go to the board and write your favorite food and your favorite color on the board.

Get a tissue, wave it in the air twice, and give it to someone wearing a blue shirt.

Get your backpack, hug it, and put it on your teacher's chair.

Walk over to a friend, say something nice to him/her and sit down beside him/her.

Turn around in a circle three times, snap your fingers and skip to your seat.

Turn the classroom light off, come to the reading area and show me what it looks like to be a good listener.

Personal Space Camp

Book: *Personal Space Camp* by Julia Cook

Publisher: National Center for Youth Issues

Grade Levels: K-2

Setting: Small Group, Classroom

Book Description

Young Louis is a space expert. He knows everything there is to know about planets, comets and spaceships. However, with all of his excitement and energy, he has difficulty remaining in his own personal space. When his teacher sends him to the principal's Personal Space Camp for the day, Louis quickly discovers that they will not be learning about the Milky Way or Saturn's rings. Through various hands-on activities, he learns important lessons about personal space and leaves camp as a certified personal space expert!

Materials Needed

- *Extension Activity #1 - hula hoops (one for each student)*
- *Extension Activity #2 - hula hoops (one for each student), radio or CD player*
- *Activity with Reproducible - photocopies of Personal Space Camp certificate (preferably on cardstock paper)*

Preparation

- *Extension Activities #1 and #2 - If your classroom is small, you will want to take students to the gymnasium or playground. Make these arrangements prior to the lesson.*

Introduction

Invite children to come to the reading area. Ask them to raise their hand if they like outer space. Ask them to raise their hand if they think they would like to travel to space one day. Display the front cover of the book and explain to students that you are going to read a book about a little boy who loves outer space. As they listen to the book, they will realize that Louis has to learn a lesson about a different kind of "space."

Follow-up Questions (after reading)

1. What made the teacher use her "cranky voice" with Louis? Have teachers (or parents) ever used their "cranky voices" with you? How did it make you feel? How do you think Louis felt?

2. Do you think Louis meant to hurt his friends' bodies when he collided with them? If not, then what made him run into them?

3. What is personal space (the area around you that keeps you safe)? Why do you think it is important?

4. Is it ever okay for someone to come into your personal space? What kinds of touches are safe? Who do you allow into your personal space?

5. Do you think Louis had fun at Personal Space Camp even though he wasn't learning about comets and spaceships? What clues did you get from the book?

6. Is it important for everyone to have personal space in the classroom? Explain.

Extension Activities

1. Hand out a hula hoop to each student and ask students to spread out so their hula hoop isn't touching anyone else's hula hoop. Explain that another word for personal space is "body bubble." This hula hoop represents their body bubble, the space around them that keeps them safe. Tell the students that they will be playing a game that will help them identify their classmates' body bubbles. If students do not know how to play Red Light, Green Light, explain the directions. Tell them that when you say Green Light, they should move around the room holding their hula hoops, but that their hula hoop should not touch anyone else's hula hoop. If it does, they must sit down on the floor in their hula hoop. When you say Red Light, they must freeze in their place. If anyone continues to move, they must sit down. Reinforce the idea that they must move in another direction as soon as they start to get close to their classmates' body bubbles.

2. Play "Musical Hoops" as a variation of Musical Chairs. Arrange hoops in a circle, so that there is a small space between each hoop. Make sure that there is one less hoop than child. When the music stops, the last child to sit in a hoop comes out of the circle and is allowed to control the music for the next round. Play until there are only two students left in the game.

Activity with Reproducible

Distribute the Personal Space Camp word find. Allow students to work in pairs, but remind them to be respectful of their partner's body bubble. When the class finishes their word find, hold a graduation ceremony and award each student with a Personal Space Camp Certificate.

Personal Space Camp Word Find

Directions: *Find the hidden words in the puzzle.*

```
T J Z I A I H Y R D V L Q X X
C P O B Z S D P T O A N Y K R
E B V T J H F U N N W N Z C D
P Z A R O A T P O T H T N K Y
S W Y E Y I I S C D B F O S P
E F Z P L U R P O O H A L U H
R W P X A E U S P A C E U L B
E F M E P F K Y E N J J H L I
T U L E E C I O V Y K N A R C
B U H C B J F B O J Z Z O M M
B Y Y A P U O O E D R S W B G
F U C P S D B I I C E Y X M T
X X Z S Y C U B L O U I S T D
X T D O A N U B L O Z C E M U
H Y D D V A G Z U E T H L Y W
```

WORD BANK

BODY BUBBLE	CRANKY VOICE	HULA HOOP
LOUIS	PERSONAL SPACE	RESPECT	SPACE EXPERT

_____

(Name)

Has Successfully Graduated From Personal Space Camp on

_____

(Date)

Congratulations on a Job Well Done!

_____

(Evaluator's Signature)

Additional Resources

Anger/Conflict Resolution

Anger's Way Out by Karen Biron-Dekel (K-5)

Every Time I Blow My Top I Lose My Head – by Lawrence Shapiro (K-5)

When I Feel Angry by Cornelia Maude Spelman & Nancy Cote (K-4)

When Sophie Gets Angry – Really, Really Angry… by Molly Bang (K-2)

Anxiety/Worrying

A Boy and a Bear by Lori Lite (K-5)

New Kid on the Block by Jodi Baldwin (K-5)

Bullying/Relational Aggression

Bully by Judith Caseley (1-4)

Bully B.E.A.N.S. by Julia Cook (1-4)

Miranda Peabody and the Magnificent Friendship March by Susan Debell, Ph.D. (K-4)

Say Something by Peggy Moss (2-5)

The Recess Queen by Alexis O'Neill and Laura Huliska-Beith (1-4)

Celebrating Differences

A Friend Like Ed by Karen Wagner (1-4)

Hooway For Wodney Wat by Helen Lester (K-3)

Who is in Your Family by Susan Bowman, Ed.S., LPC (K-4)

Cooperation/Sharing

Have You Filled a Bucket Today? by Carol McCloud (K-5)

That's Mine! Keep Your Hands Off (Good Citizenship Counts Series) by Linda Hagler, M.Ed. (K-5)

Additional Resources

Feelings

How Are You Peeling? by Saxton Freymann (K-2)

Hurty Feelings by Helen Lester (K-2)

My Many Colored Days by Dr. Seuss (K-3)

The Magic Coloring Book of Feelings by Robert P. Bowman, Ph.D. and Kim (Tip) Frank, Ed.S., LPC (K-5)

The Way I Feel by Janan Cain (K-5)

Friendship

Don't Need Friends by Carolyn Crimi (K-3)

How to Be a Friend by Laurie and Marc Brown (K-2)

Miranda Peabody Learns What It Takes to Make New Friends by Susan DeBell, Ph.D. (K-4)

Say Hello by Jack & Michael Foreman (K-3)

Goal-Setting/Persevering

Horton Hatches the Egg by Dr. Seuss (1-5)

How Grinner Became a Winner by Robert Bowman, Ph.D. & John Chanaca, Ed.D. (K-5)

Honesty

Princess K.I.M and the Lie That Grew by Maryann Cocca-Leffler (K-3)

Ruthie and the (Not So) Teeny Tiny Lie by Laura Rankin (K-3)

Sam Tells Stories by Thierry Robberecht (1-3)

The Best Story Ever (Good Citizenship Counts Series) by Linda Hagler, M.Ed. (K-5)

The Honest-to-Goodness-Truth by Patricia McKissack (2-5)

Additional Resources

Respect/Manners/Empathy

Do Unto Otters: A Book About Manners by Laurie Keller (K-3)

Dude, That's Rude! (Laugh and Learn Series) by Pamela Espeland & Elizabeth Verdick (3-6)

Whoopi's Big Book of Manners by Whoopi Goldberg (K-3)

Rumors

Miranda Peabody and the Case of the Lunchroom Spy by Susan DeBell, Ph.D. (K-4)

Self-Esteem

Edward the Emu by Sheena Knowles (K-3)

Giraffes Can't Dance by Giles Andreae (K-3)

Hooray for You! by Marianne Richmond (K-5)

Howard B. Wigglebottom Listens to His Heart by Howard Binkow (K-3)

I'm Gonna Like Me: Letting off a Little Self-Esteem by Jamie Lee Curtis (K-3)

I Like Myself by Karen Beaumont (K-4)

Social Skills

Howard B. Wigglebottom Learns to Listen by Howard Binkow (K-3)

It's Hard to Be Five: Learning How to Work My Control Panel by Jamie Lee Curtis (K-2)

Me First by Helen Lester (K-3)

My Mouth Is A Volcano by Julia Cook (1-4)

The Tattle Tail Tale by Tandy Braid (K-3)

References

Agnes, S.M. (1946). Bibliotherapy for Socially Maladjusted Children. *Catholic Educational Review*, 44, 8-16.

Iaquinta, A. & Hipsky, S. (2006). Practical Bibliotherapy Strategies for the Inclusive Elementary Classroom. *Early Childhood Education Journal*, 34, 209-213.

Pehrsson, D.E., Allen, V.B., Folger, W.A., McMillen, P.S., & Lowe, I. (2007). Bibliotherapy With Preadolescents Experiencing Divorce. *The Family Journal*, 15, 409-414.

Prater, M.A., Johnstun, M.L., Dyches, T.T., Johnstun, M.R. (2006). Using Children's Books as Bibliotherapy for At-Risk Students: A Guide for Teachers. *Preventing School Failure,* 50, 5-13.

Rycik, M.T. (2006). 9/11 to the Iraq War: Using Books to Help Children Understand Troubled Times. *Childhood Education,* 82, 145-152.

Sullivan, A.K. & Strang, H.R. (2002/2003). Bibliotherapy in the Classroom: Using Literature to Promote the Development of Emotional Intelligence. *Childhood Education,* 79, 74-80.

About the Authors

Kate Brambrut, M.A., NCC, received her B.A. degree in magazine journalism from the University of Georgia. After working for several education based non-profit agencies in Atlanta and Washington D.C., she returned to school to earn her Master's Degree in School Counseling from George Washington University. Kate began her school counseling career in Fairfax County Public Schools in Virginia, where she worked for several years as an elementary school counselor. She is currently working toward completing her LPC certification, with the ultimate goal of opening a counseling center for low income children and families. She loves working with students every day and she is passionate about the crucial role that literature can play in helping children cope with problems they are facing. Kate is currently working as a middle school counselor in Atlanta, Georgia, where she lives with her husband, 2-year old son and infant daughter.

Amy E. Sauder Lehman, M.A., NCC, LPC, received her B.S. degree in elementary education from Eastern Mennonite University in Harrisonburg, Virginia. After teaching fourth grade in the Washington D.C. public school system for several years, she earned her Master's Degree in School Counseling from George Washington University. While serving as a school counselor, she worked toward her Licensed Professional Counselor certificate, which she acquired in 2007. In the past several years, Amy has enjoyed supervising graduate interns at GW and giving various workshops on Bibliotherapy. She is a Nursery – 8th grade counselor at Holy Trinity School in Washington, D.C. Amy lives in Alexandria, Virginia, with her husband and son.